HouseBeautiful

STYLE SECRETS

WHAT EVERY ROOM NEEDS

SOPHIE DONELSON

ABRAMS, NEW YORK

CONTENTS

INTRODUCTION
BY SOPHIE DONELSON

LONG BEFORE I JOINED *House Beautiful*, I was a subscriber, eagerly tearing out pages of lush bedrooms, sun-drenched breakfast nooks, and inventive color palettes—pages that set my heart aflutter. What made me a loyal reader then is still what delights me behind the editor's desk: the feeling of being just one photograph, quote, or caption away from an aesthetic awakening, or at least a prettier tomorrow.

"Are you a decorating pro by now? How incredible is your home?" I'm often asked. Don't be ridiculous! I'm a perpetual student, soaking in tips from top decorators right alongside my readers. But since I see the rough cut—thousands of gorgeous rooms before the handful culled for primetime—I will admit to seeing a few patterns emerge. Indeed, there are things most decorators agree every room needs.

An overscale urn or plant or painting for gravitas. Luminosity, be it with a crystal chandelier or a single mirror. A punch of black. This book shares dozens of them, all shortcuts for surefire success in every and any home.

And note this: There's no budget required for entry. Since *House Beautiful*'s founding in 1896, we've engaged our readers with ideas to *try*, not just things to *buy*. A smart reader walks away with scores of potential new home upgrades in each issue—no shopping required.

Thanks to this book, my to-do list is mounting (pages 88 and 33 are first—and, someday, 18!). What will you try?

And speaking of thanks, I had plenty of help on this book: my talented predecessor and mentor, Newell Turner, *House Beautiful* creative director Eleftherios Kardamakis, and interiors editor Doretta Sperduto, whose loving touch and exquisite flowers light up nearly every page. Gratitude to Hearst Books sherpa Jacqueline Deval, my editor Rebecca Kaplan, and photo editor Martha Corcoran, too. Thank you to our legion of incredible designers, photographers, and stylists. And many thanks to Lisa Cregan, whose storytelling continues to educate and entertain the discerning *HB* audience—myself included.

Now get ready to get inspired and get busy. There are eight things every room needs—but it only takes one to change your point of view.

CHAPTER I

EVERY ROOM NEEDS A SPLASH OF UNEXPECTED COLOR

• • •

THINK OF A RAINBOW AS A METAPHOR FOR DECORATING. ALL THE COLORS IN THE WORLD ARE OUT THERE WAITING. IT JUST TAKES A BIT OF MAGIC TO BRING THEM OUT.

OPPOSITE Who'd have guessed that lavender walls, not white, not cream, could calm the riot of color in this Park Avenue living room?

LEFT A pair of Edward Wormley armchairs upholstered in tangerine is the last thing expected in a white, crisp, and beachy Nantucket living room. Since orange and blue are opposites on the color wheel, the mirror provides show-stopping contrast.

ABOVE Pops of orange against navy blue walls have the stimulating effect of a double espresso. The tangerine border on white curtains draws the eye up and creates a sense of height in this standard-sized bedroom.

CLOCKWISE FROM TOP LEFT A painting by Karyn Lyons brings a surreal flavor to a sunny breakfast nook in Michigan. A stroke of vibrant color animates a neutral living room. A beach house façade displays unflinching chromatic courage with big splashes of tangerine. An empty bookcase painted orange sets off fiery sparks.

Orange accents are calypso lively by day and glowing and mellow at night on this upstairs veranda in a Bahamian getaway house. The tangerine and white palette strikes the right balance for an adult refuge that doubles as a rainy day hangout for the homeowners' two young sons.

A PAINTED FLOOR

A MARBLE checkerboard or a sea-like swath of blue; a painted floor presents promising new possibilities underfoot.

OPPOSITE A white chevron pattern painted over an ebony-stained floor in this Manhattan apartment foyer creates a welcome surprise right at the threshold.

THIS PAGE A painted motif inspired by the folk-art hex signs that decorate Pennsylvania Dutch Country barns embellishes the living room floor of this farmhouse.

In this diminutive Manhattan apartment, the foyer triples as dining room and library. The faux-marble painted floor (along with tomato-red walls!) gives it a sense of importance.

CLOCKWISE FROM TOP LEFT A previously unassuming entry brims with personality with a geometric painted floor. In a tiny Manhattan apartment the painted floor mimics a rug for a clean feel. Coats of aqua paint maintain authenticity in this new summerhouse bathroom in Maine. An upstairs dining room opens to an outdoor porch, so the floor is painted to look like stone.

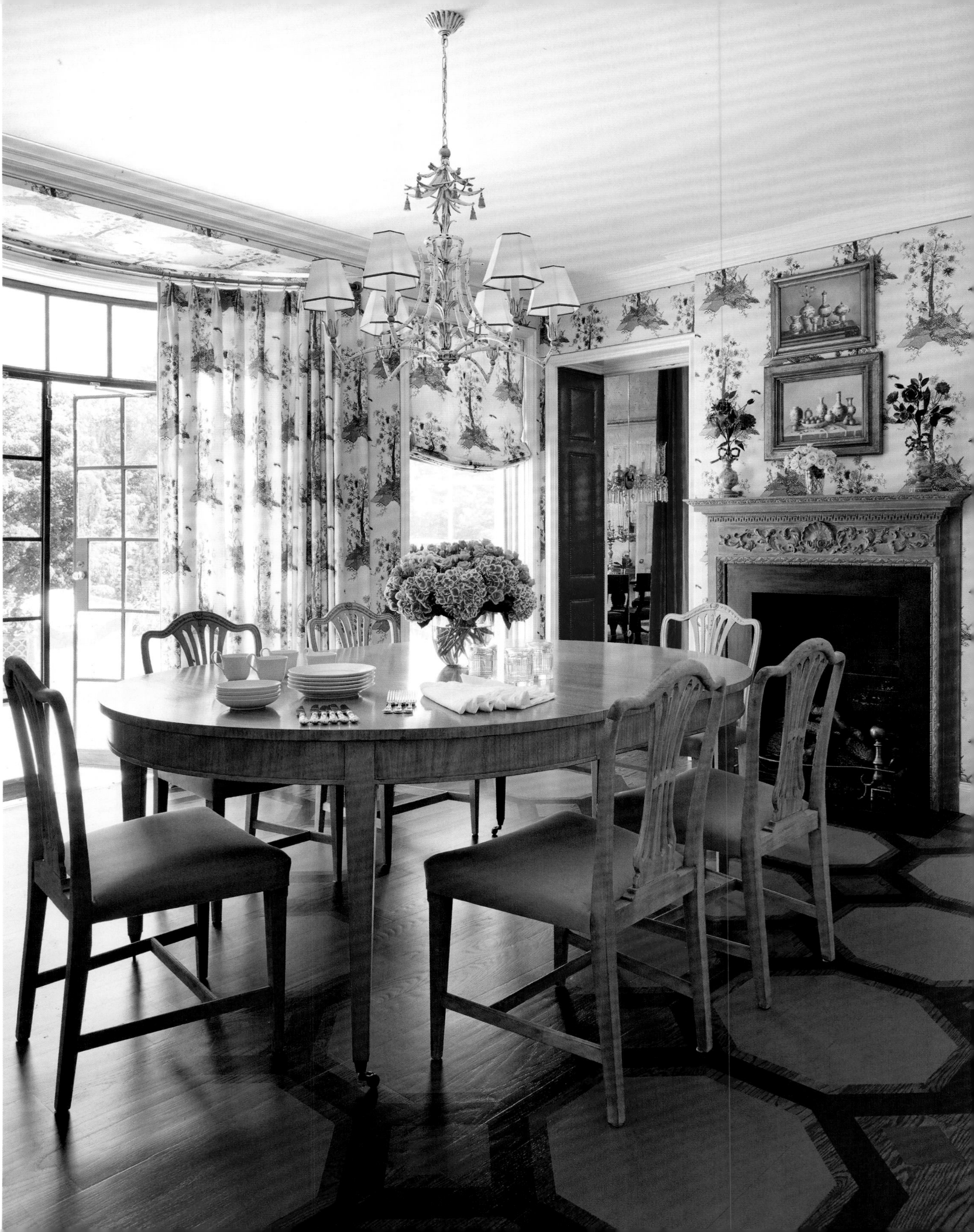

OPPOSITE A traditional octagonal honeycomb pattern has a youthful attitude when blown up to large scale and painted on a breakfast room floor in shades of electric blue.

THIS PAGE All it takes is a checkerboard floor in an eye-catching hue to add dazzle to an ordinary white kitchen. The combination of the orange floor and the blue door makes a powerful statement.

A brilliant shade of green was pulled from this Manhattan bedroom's silk wallcovering for valances, the headboard, and stools. It's an intimate refuge that leaves the blaring city far behind.

Bright purple striped pillows are an even livelier accent inside the neutral background of this beach house living room. The pattern on bent-wood armchairs has just enough plum to pull the color across the room.

THE NASHER COLLECTION

OPPOSITE Rich purple and blue tones drawn from the antique Khotan rug add depth to a San Francisco living room and give this new renovation a settled feel.

THIS PAGE Purple and green are two complementary colors that seem to have been made for each other—think Wimbledon! In a man's study, a Chinese art deco rug harmonizes with the olive-check wallcovering.

In a master bedroom, peacock-blue walls complement a sprinkling of purples. The color of the bed's tiger velvet bolster is reiterated on the swoop-arm chair across the room.

IKAT AND SUZANI LOVE

THE WORD *IKAT* comes from the Malaysian *mengikat*, meaning "to dye," and it's long been a popular style in Southeast Asia, where weavers tie loose threads into bundles for dyeing. The difficult task of color-matching those dyed threads prior to weaving a pattern is what gives an ikat its signature slightly blurry look.

Suzani's origins are more Central Asian than ikat's, and the word comes from the Persian for "needle," so think of suzanis as needlework. By tradition, the pieces are part of a bride's dowry and young Tajik, Uzbek, and Kazakh women have been chain-stitching native-inspired motifs like suns, moons, flowers, and fish onto cotton backing since Marco Polo was working the Silk Road.

OPPOSITE When used in this powder room, a silk ikat wall-covering's large-scale print seems energizing rather than overwhelming.

THIS PAGE Could there be a simpler or more stunning solution for a guest room headboard? Just casually tie a suzani to hooks on the wall for a relaxed and colorful look.

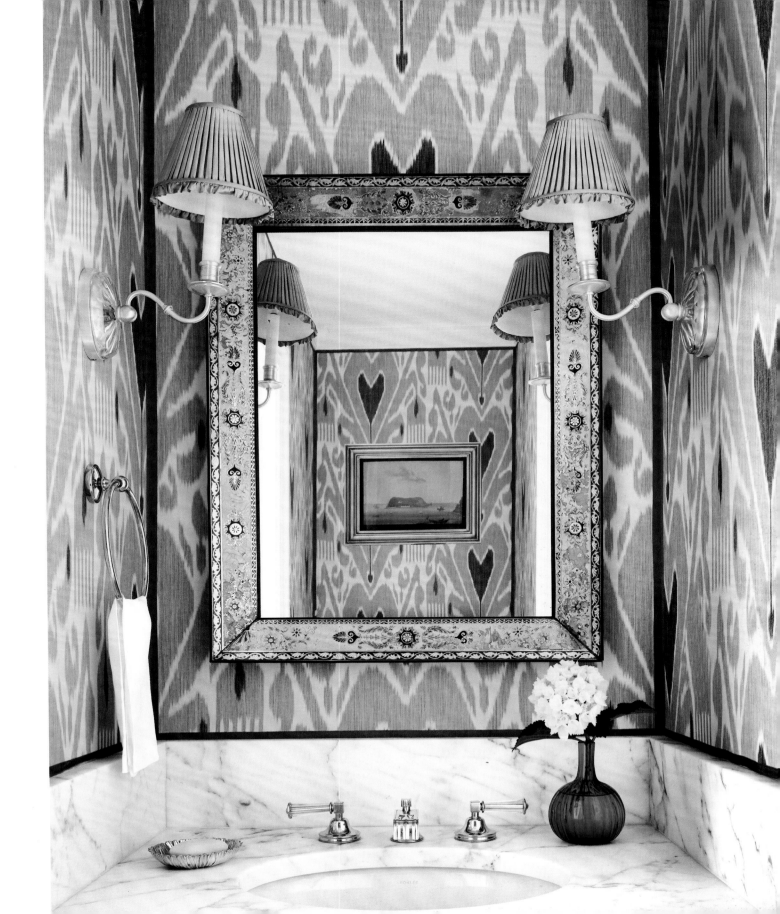

THIS PAGE In a living room filled with bold gestures, the most audacious choice is a sofa upholstered in an overscale ikat print. Its companion red sofa is strewn with pillows in both ikat and suzani patterns.

OPPOSITE FROM TOP A green ikat on a settee turns up the volume in an otherwise neutral living room. A well-traveled atmosphere is conveyed when a Los Angeles bedroom's walls are covered in exotic fabric. A blue-and-white ikat print freshens a traditional bedroom.

BORDERLINE MADNESS

PAINT YOUR moldings
or muntins a color (no, not
white!) to outline your room
like a frame does a painting.

OPPOSITE Tall cobalt-blue baseboards outline a Manhattan dining room and set off walls sheathed in turquoise silk.

THIS PAGE Mornings in this summerhouse breakfast area are always cheery because the sun shines in through panes of glass with orange-painted muntins.

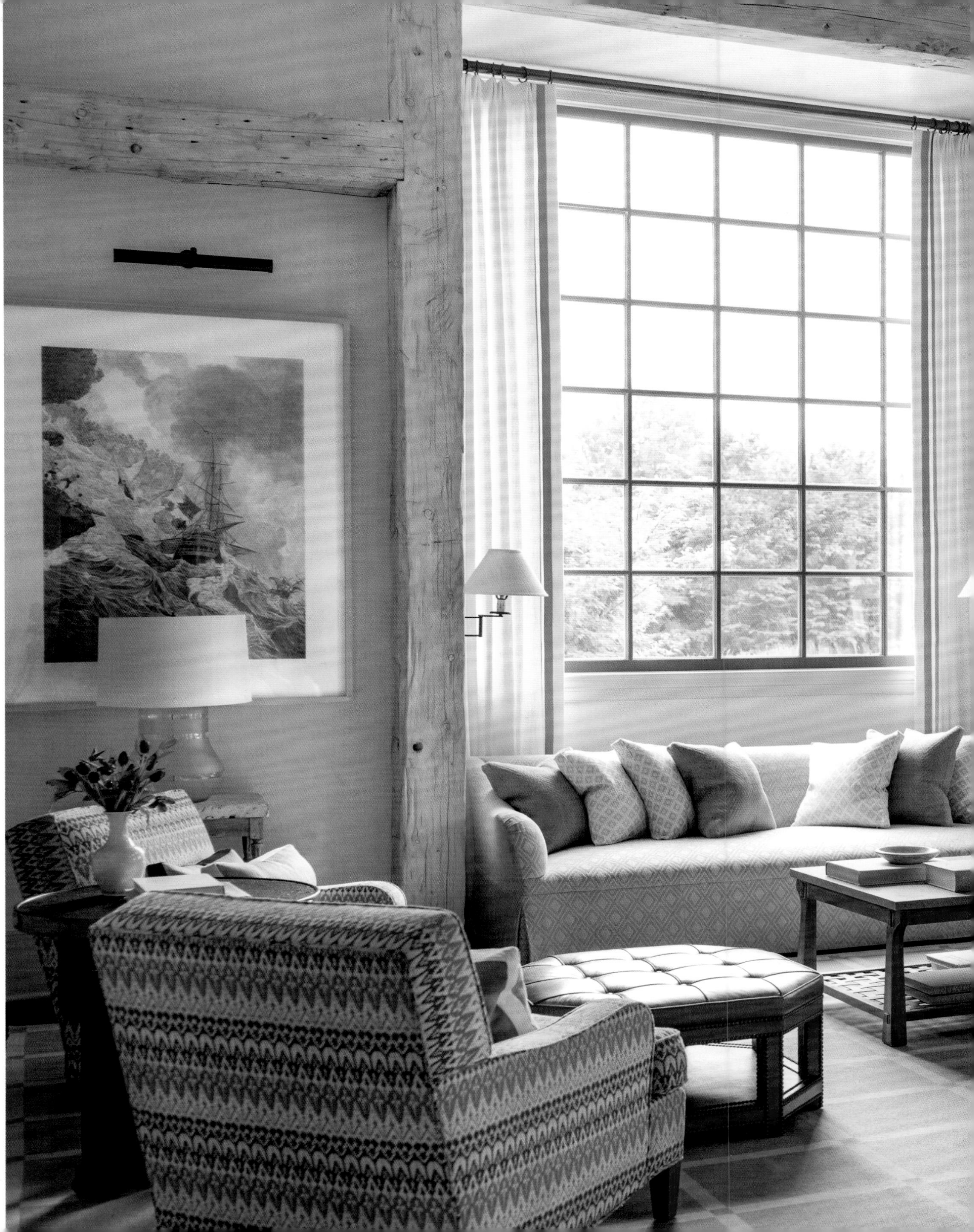

Windows and French doors in this double-height living room are painted to match the ribbon trim on the curtains and draw the eye to the sylvan landscape outside.

CHAPTER II

EVERY ROOM NEEDS A NOD TO THE PAST

• • •

THE FUNNY THING ABOUT CLASSICS IS

THEY ALWAYS LOOK RIGHT. WHY NOT FIND A SPOT

TO MIX IN A BLAST FROM CENTURIES PAST?

GREAT LOOKS ENDURE FOR A REASON.

OPPOSITE Inspired by eighteenth-century Caribbean plantations, the great room in this Bahamas house exudes gracious ease. A classic blue-and-white palette and coral stone walls are striking counterpoints to the floor, stained to look like mahogany.

Showcasing the power of symmetry, a key tenet of classicism, two matching English-style bookcases painted taupe regally flank a living room fireplace. A pair of Klismos chairs reinforces the sense of balance.

Nothing can jar the serenity
of this Manhattan living room.
Strict symmetry maintains
the visual peace, and the wall
color keeps things feeling airy
and atmospheric.

THE LATE Finnish-born designer Eero Saarinen's determination to "clear up the slum of legs in the U.S. home" led to the 1956 creation of his now iconic Pedestal Table, inspired, he said, by the image of a falling drop of highly viscous liquid. Manufacturer Knoll Studio stamps the underside of every table with the signature of the artist, treating them as the sculptural masterpieces they are. Though Saarinen made numerous contributions to the pantheon of modern design, none is so firmly fixed in popular culture as the Pedestal Table, whose simple elegance seems to suit every style of décor. Today we call it simply "a Saarinen table."

A black Saarinen table offers sleek contrast to the traditional scrollwork of Queen Anne–style chairs in this dining room.

CLOCKWISE FROM TOP LEFT The shock of chartreuse chairs paired with a modernist table brings a playful spirit to a formal dining room. As if to emphasize its contribution to yin and yang, a Saarinen table is topped with a fragment of a Buddhist temple. An explosion of candy-store pastels in this kitchen is calmed by the purity of the table. A vintage Saarinen table enlivens an intimate spot for family meals.

For a young Manhattan couple who love to entertain, a Saarinen table paired with a long banquette makes practical sense—extra people can squeeze in, and if someone happens to spill red wine, it wipes right up.

TRADITIONAL ENGLISH FLORALS (THEY'RE CHIC AGAIN!)

OPPOSITE Entering this pink-lacquered parlor through the passage created by a pair of flowery chairs is as uplifting as walking past a perennial border in full bloom.

THIS PAGE Dining room curtains are in a classic floral fabric, but with a youthful, updated black-and-white palette that feels fresh.

In this nineteenth-century house with magnificent gardens, the striped chairs effectively bring the landscape's earthy colors into the dining room.

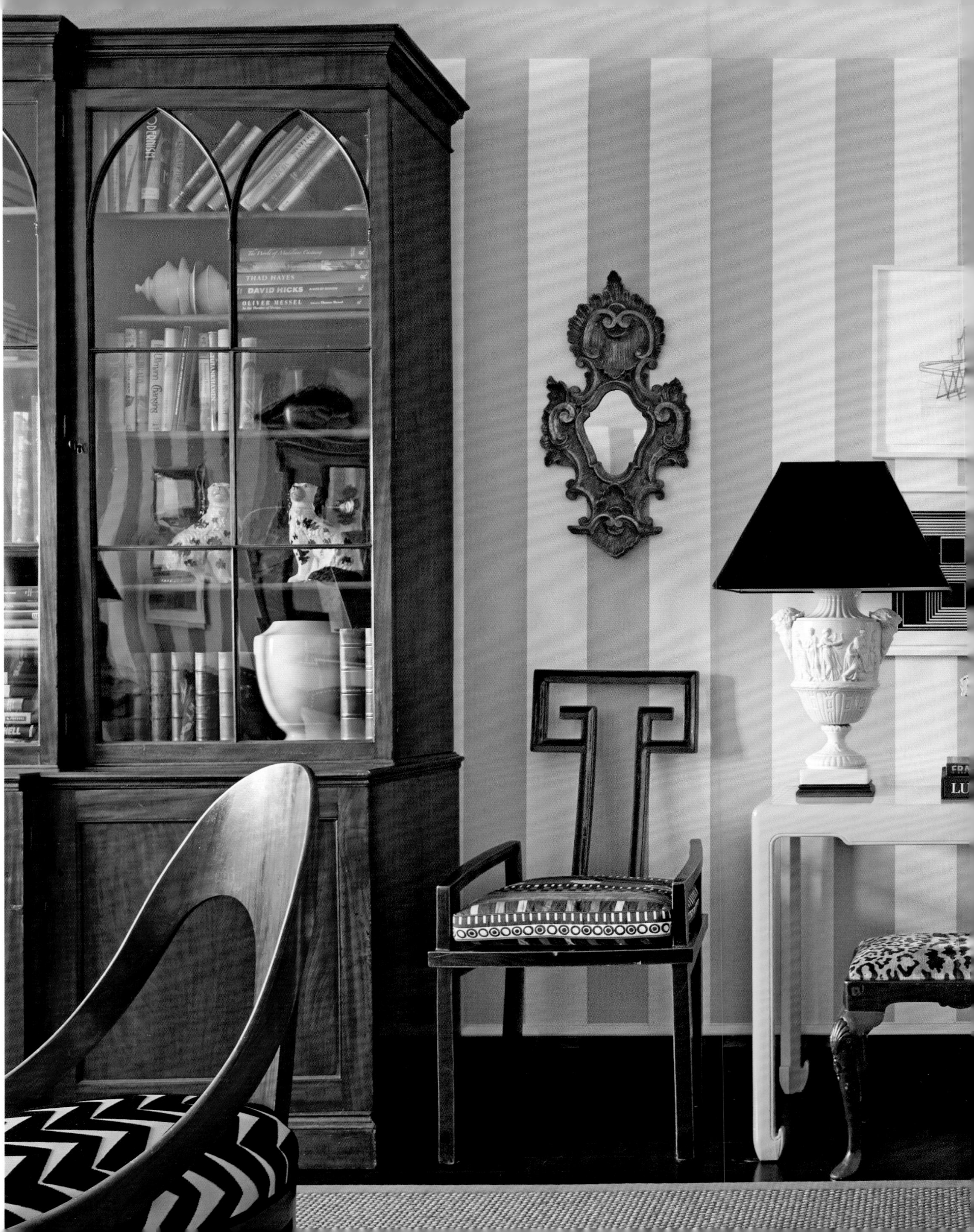
THAD HAYES
DAVID HICKS
OLIVER MESSEL

Walls painted to resemble awning stripes create a backdrop just as interesting as the eye-popping shots of color and contemporary art collection in this Manhattan living room.

GOOD JEFFERSONIAN WHITE

OUR DESIGN-minded third president, Thomas Jefferson, looked to the classical architecture of France and Greece for inspiration, leading to his liberal use of what decorator Michael S. Smith once called "good Jeffersonian white" at Monticello and the University of Virginia.

OPPOSITE Family photos in matching black frames pop against white walls in this narrow hallway.

THIS PAGE Pristine white walls against a checkerboard marble floor, presided over by a coordinating staircase in high-contrast black and white, create an MGM musical moment in this glamorous foyer.

A voluminous great room's varied ceiling heights are unified by white. The bleached, skeletal look of the room plays up the celestial chandelier over the dining table. Even the pale wood furniture, which might have been lost with another wall color, stands out.

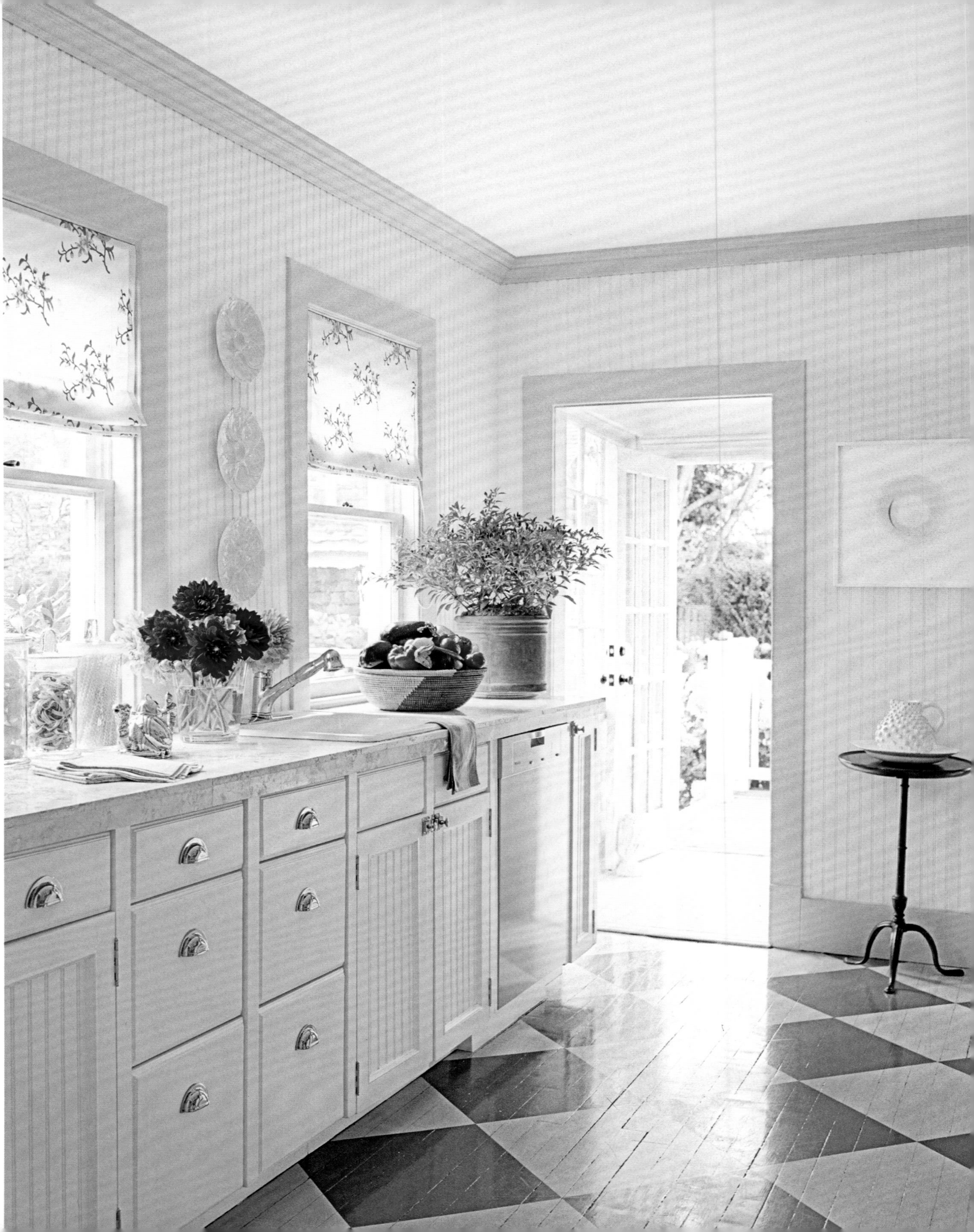

OPPOSITE Existing beadboard cabinets in this vintage kitchen were refreshed with crisp white paint, and the floor was animated by a classic checkerboard pattern.

THIS PAGE White-painted plank cabinetry with painted hinges and black latches gives this brand-new kitchen some old-fashioned charm.

CHAPTER III

EVERY ROOM NEEDS
A GRAND GESTURE

• • •

GO BIG AND GO HOME! ISN'T IT TIME YOU MADE

A STATEMENT, A REALLY BIG STATEMENT?

OVERSCALE IS NOT THE SAME AS OVERDONE.

OPPOSITE A colossal ceramic vase literally overflowing with flowering branches is placed on a coffee table to underscore the verdant look and uninhibited warmth of this sunny living room.

A circa-1740 Chippendale mirror makes a spectacular focal point at a Long Island weekend house. Its magnificence distracts from the humble plank walls of the place, which was originally a garage.

THIS PAGE An eccentric purple mirror in an entry offers a cheery greeting to the visitor coming off the gray streets of Manhattan. Its jewel-tone frame surrounds the mirror like a chunky amethyst necklace.

OPPOSITE A four-foot-tall mirror takes the place of a picture window in a previously dark apartment entry—the mother-of-pearl inlay mimics moldings and a sill.

CLOCKWISE FROM TOP LEFT A dramatic dining room mirror was cleverly constructed from an antique stone overdoor and mirrored squares of old glass. Twelve-foot ceilings and an eight-foot-long sofa call for a large-scale starburst mirror. A fantastically ornate Chippendale giltwood mirror reflects a vivid Joan Mitchell diptych. A convex mirror expands the boundaries of a dining room.

A vast forest unfolds outside this bedroom, so a stunning hexagonal citron-color mirror was hung in front of the window to hold the occupant's gaze, safe and protected inside the room.

A GIGANTIC URN

FILL IT WITH with seasonal blooms, fill it with clementines. Who needs a centerpiece when there's an oversize garden urn holding court in the room?

. . . .

THIS PAGE To avoid the spiritually dead and all-too-ubiquitous "seldom-used" feeling in a formal dining room, the focus here is on life—live greenery, that is—with fig branches arranged loosely in a rugged bronze urn.

OPPOSITE Chartreuse walls stand like a privet hedge behind a large garden urn. The space feels more like a secret garden than a suburban dining room, and the urn provides graphic presence in a room busy with pattern.

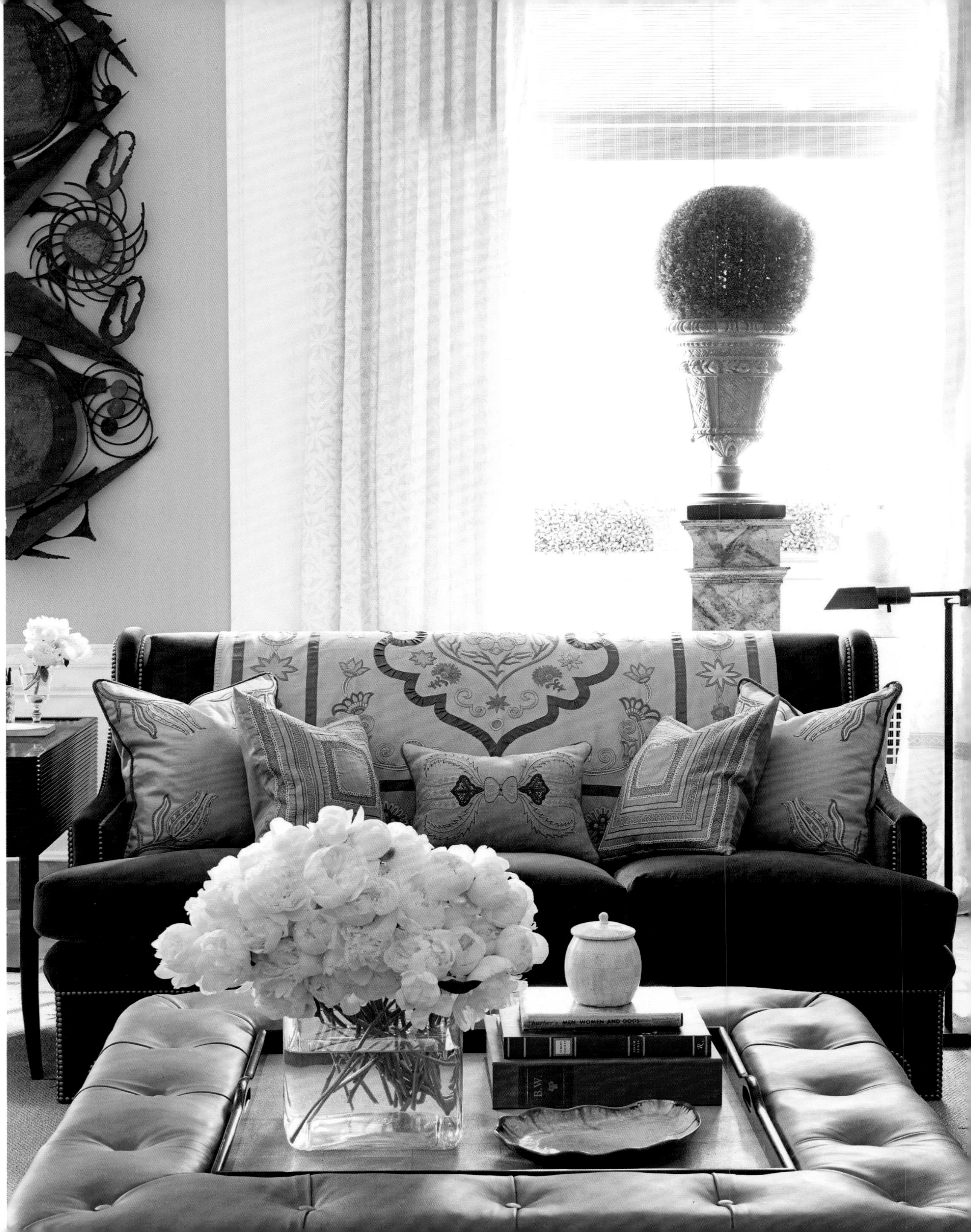
Thurber's MEN WOMEN AND DOGS
B.W.

OPPOSITE The large urn on a marble plinth adds the dignity of antiquity to the flamboyant colors and designs in this living room. It also draws the eye upward from a low-slung sofa.

THIS PAGE It's no small surprise to open the powder room door and be greeted by a garden urn reinvented as the sink!

THE FOUR-POSTER BED. When Shakespeare died, he famously left his wife, Anne, only his "second-best bed," a seemingly meager bequest that's generated lots of academic conjecture about the state of their marriage. But Elizabethan-era beds were often a serious store of wealth—with elaborately carved headboards, gold-embroidered bedding, and four sturdy, sometimes jewel-encrusted, posters. Those posters supported a roof frame called a "tester," hung with heavy drapery that provided sleepers both privacy and protection from the dank drafts of sixteenth-century homes. As indoor heating evolved, so too did the four-poster bed. First to go were the velvet drapes; then the posters themselves became gradually slimmer and more elegant as their utility shifted to supporting more purely decorative fabrics—if any at all.

. . . .

A mahogany bed with commanding British Colonial style brings human scale to this room with a grand cathedral ceiling. It was custom-carved in India with a whimsical pineapple at the top of each of its four posters.

THIS PAGE Ebony walls set off a magnificent bed with a voluminous canopy and lavish hangings in this extravagant master bedroom.

OPPOSITE A canopy bed creates an inner sanctuary in a master bedroom where a swan painting hung on mirrors makes the entire experience seem a happy dream.

In a nod to "old Britannia" or maybe an homage to the Raj, a chinoiserie daybed inspired by eighteenth-century Chippendale designs dominates a library where wallpaper panels depict scenes of colonial India.

CLOCKWISE FROM TOP LEFT A bedskirt softens this steel four-poster bed, and its straight lines play off curvy painted vines on the walls. A tailored pinstripe canopy and navy blue walls declare this bedroom a masculine haven. A master bedroom is infused with a cool shade of gray-blue taken from the metal bed. Channeling the great English country house bedrooms, painted faux-horn bedposts support a cream-colored silk canopy.

A library's floor space is almost completely consumed by a U-shaped sofa. Its upholstery is closely matched to the wall color for a jewel-box effect. The sofa was conceived for teenagers to pile on and watch movies; the kids have dubbed it "Big Blue."

A plush banquette spans an entire wall—not an everyday sight in a glass-box city apartment like this—but its luxurious appeal creates coziness in spite of the chilly glass walls. For unity, pale blue upholstery merges with views of expansive sky.

A table abuts this roomy kitchen island, creating scads of additional prep space. The efficient arrangement allows a chef to prepare dinner and enjoy guests all at once.

LEFT This turquoise kitchen island has the look of an old-time brass-latch icebox. Its countertop is concrete poured to resemble the wooden slats of a picnic table. Utilitarian? Yes, but fun too.

ABOVE A massive circa-1890 Flemish table acts as a surprisingly bold island. (The designer added the brass accents.) It's illuminated by pendants that resemble the rotund details of its legs.

A HANGING LIGHT FIT FOR A CASTLE

WITH A massive light fixture directing the attention overhead, you hardly have to bother with decorating the rest of the room at all.

OPPOSITE Low ceilings were no deterrent to choosing this gigantic pendant light. The antique lantern gives the low-slung dining room a romantic grotto atmosphere.

THIS PAGE A slender, elongated lantern fits inside the arch of window moldings in this yawning, barn-like staircase hall.

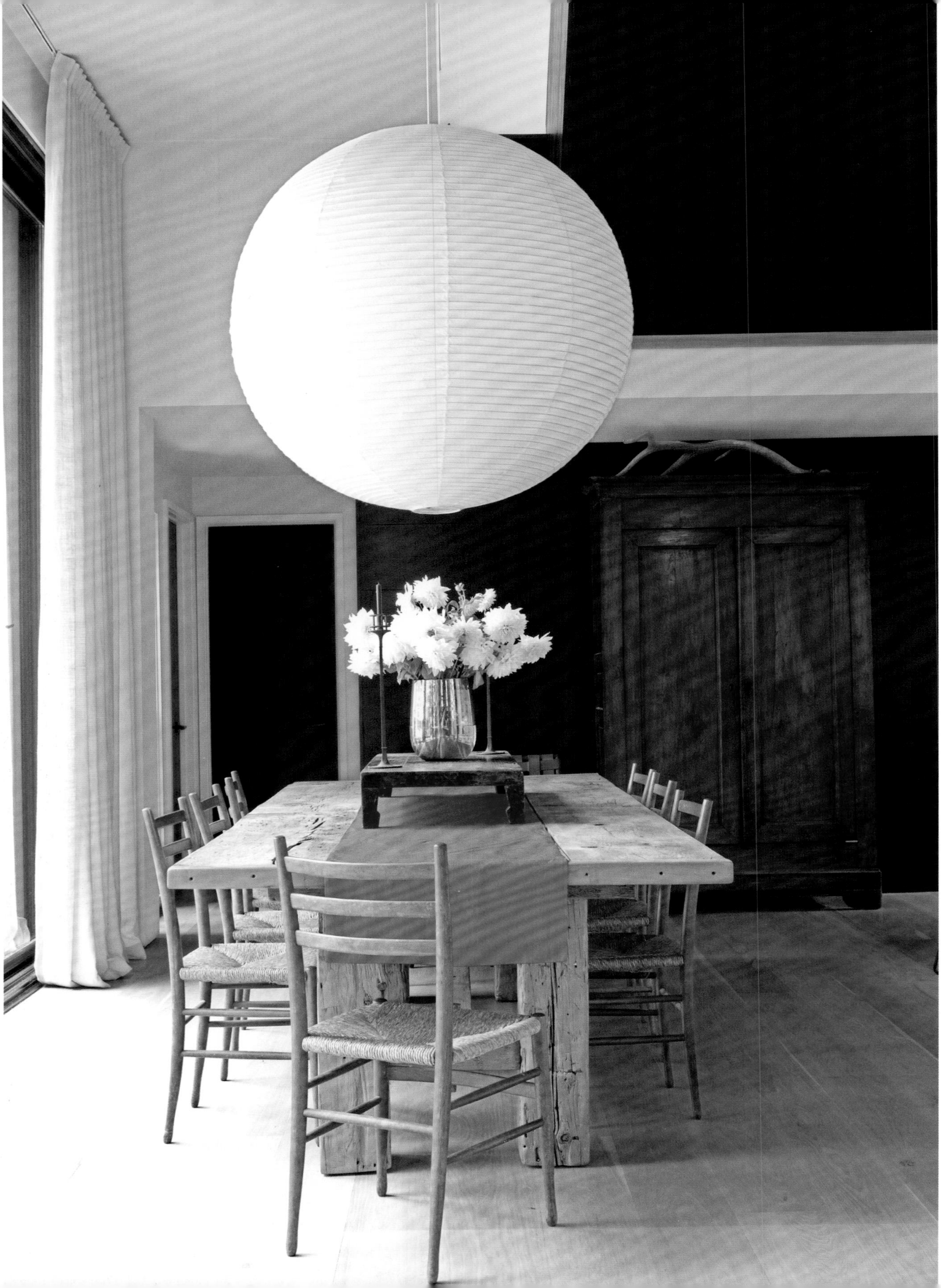

OPPOSITE An extra-large Noguchi lantern hovers like a full moon, casting a warm glow and creating an intimate dining spot in a cavernous open-plan great room.

THIS PAGE A glorious mass of translucent bubbles floats above this dining table, giving a 1940s-era house a whole new attitude.

COCO CHANEL   JUSTINE PICARDIE

Bert Morgan   Young Jackie   Viking Studio

SHABBY CHIC   RACHEL ASHWELL   ASSOULINE

A PRIVILEGED LIFE   ASSOULINE

VOGUE LIVING HOUSES, GARDENS, PEOPLE

Diana   THE PORTRAIT   ROSALIND COWARD   FOREWORD NELSON MANDELA

FLOWERS   CAROLYNE ROEHM

Duncan   PICASSO & LUMP   Bulfinch

THE PERFECTLY IMPERFECT HOME   DEBORAH NEEDLEMAN

Hung and Hagberg   By Hand

I ♥ Your Style   Amanda Brooks

CAMPBELL/SEEBOHM   ELSIE DE WOLFE: A DECORATIVE LIFE   POTTER

CAROLYN RANCE   JON J MUTH   *A Family of Poems*

IN THE SPIRIT OF   PALM BEACH   ASSOULINE

ANNIE KELLY   ROOMS TO INSPIRE   R

BEAUTY AT HOME   AERIN LAUDER

CARRIER AND COMPANY   POSITIVELY CHIC INTERIORS

ANNIE KELLY   ROOMS TO INSPIRE IN THE COUNTRY   R

Simon Evans

SWOPE/AARONS/TELLER   HOTEL IL PELLICANO

the audrey hepburn treasures

MILES REDD THE BIG BOOK OF C

THE WORLD IN VOGUE PEOPLE, PARTIES, PL

THE ROSE

CHAPTER IV

EVERY ROOM NEEDS GLITTER AND GLEAM

• • •

THE GLINT OF GOLD, THE SPARKLE OF SILVER—
WHETHER IT'S MIRRORS OR METALS, GLOSSY WALLS
OR SHIMMERING WATER, LET REFLECTED LIGHT
BRIGHTEN YOUR HOME.

OPPOSITE Sentimental mementos like children's art and a framed Fisher-Price toy
feel even more playful displayed on brilliant bubblegum-pink shelves.

LACQUER TAKES on a life of its own—walls look animated, furniture shines, and whole rooms seem flooded with romantic refractions.

. . . .

The formal front parlor in a New Orleans row house could have been a lifeless affair, but with light bouncing off its luscious lime-lacquered walls, it's radiant.

A vintage bar cabinet in a dining room provides a brightly varnished counterpart to high-sheen cherry-red walls.

CLOCKWISE FROM TOP LEFT This vintage desk had an ordinary matte-black finish before its trip to an auto-body shop, where it was spray-painted a high-gloss azure. The dining area's banquette is an exact color match to the sparkling walls, giving the shock of shine even more emphasis. A very functional hallway lined with closets becomes an impossibly handsome mudroom when painted a glassy twilight blue. A kitchen ceiling sheathed in watery teal picks up the color of iridescent tile and visually expands the room.

SHIMMERING WATER

THERE'S SOMETHING universally appealing about light shining on water. Be it rivers, lakes, oceans, or pools, man finds comfort near the water's edge.

· ·

This infinity pool might be anywhere until the mist lifts and the skyline of downtown Los Angeles materializes on the horizon.

CLOCKWISE FROM TOP LEFT A weeping willow hovers over the trickling fountain in this peaceful Charleston garden. A Hamptons swimming pool's clean lines highlight the natural charm of lush hydrangeas and privet. From their bedroom balcony, these homeowners have a view of a 1934 swimming pool and stunning boxwood parterres. Windowed French doors open to a walled garden, making this shower feel nearly alfresco.

Glimpsed through French doors, the ripples of a reflecting pool, original to this 1920s house, draw the eye to a sweeping view of the Savannah River.

CRYSTALS

THIS PAGE A flea-market candelabra and a delicate glass sconce twinkle against dark teal walls like sequins glinting on a ball gown.

OPPOSITE Everyone's skin looks radiant in a dining room where the light from a show-stopping bronze and crystal chandelier reflects off silver tea-leaf wallpaper.

The fluid lines of a vintage crystal Baguès sconce harmonize with the geometric pattern etched into a stone fireplace mantel.

CLOCKWISE FROM TOP LEFT A blockbuster 1960s Venini chandelier created from pieces of textured glass wows in this Manhattan dining room. A princely eighteenth-century crystal chandelier contrasts with simple bare floors and the sculptural lines of the chairs. An antique beaded-crystal chandelier has an ethereal quality that doesn't overpower a small dining room. Humble cottage kitchen meets worldly Parisian bistro thanks to a crystal chandelier and high-gloss black paint.

THE PHRASE "worth its weight in gold" holds true for decorating too. A little goes a long way.

. . . .

The glorious golden tones of an over-the-top 1940s French bronze desk repeat throughout this library— from a gold stool to the legs on the coffee table to the metallic colors in the curtains. Even the leather chairs are trimmed with shining brass nailheads.

A sunroom fills with an amber glow at end of day. A gilt fauteuil and the subtle shine of metallic fabrics enhance the radiance.

CLOCKWISE FROM TOP LEFT The warmth of a brass-clad kitchen island balances the cool tones of the other metals. The range's trim inspired this kitchen's brass sink fixtures, which are un-lacquered and will mellow over time. Blue and gold make a striking combination in a shower where a niche is inset with a vintage mirror. The bronze tones in this powder room's wallpaper prompted strong gold accents like the sink and faucet.

Glimmers of silver and gold spark a soft-spoken palette in this living room. The lamp is a lustrous backdrop to the owner's collection of antique silver.

CHAPTER V

EVERY ROOM NEEDS TO EMBRACE THE GREAT OUTDOORS

• • •

MOTHER NATURE'S KNOCKING. LET HER IN!

THROW OPEN YOUR HOME AND EXPERIENCE

THE NATURAL BEAUTY THAT WANDERS IN.

OPPOSITE If you want your outdoor terrace to read as cozy as an indoor room, then add a "window" complete with "window seat." The lookout point cut into this Florida terrace frames a view of living artwork that changes with the season.

SOMETHING WILD ON THE WALL

WHETHER YOU dream of tramping a dusky meadow or a forest footpath, embellish your walls with your personal Eden and live every day in a pastoral paradise.

A fantasy depiction of the owners' favorite vacation spot, Antigua, is painted on dining room walls from the viewpoint of a tropical island porch, complete with an applied wood railing and faux columns.

A wildflower meadow grows across
a wall, adding feminine verve to
a sunroom where two teenage
daughters spend time with friends.

CLOCKWISE FROM TOP LEFT This powder room feels like an enchanted garden where purple orchids twine across the walls to encompass a purple painted mirror. Glow-y gold palm tree wallpaper gives this master bedroom the feel of a tropical resort. A decorative painter embellished an otherwise nondescript foyer's grass cloth walls with a striking image of a live oak. A full-blown obsession with pink peonies is indulged in this New Jersey shore house powder room.

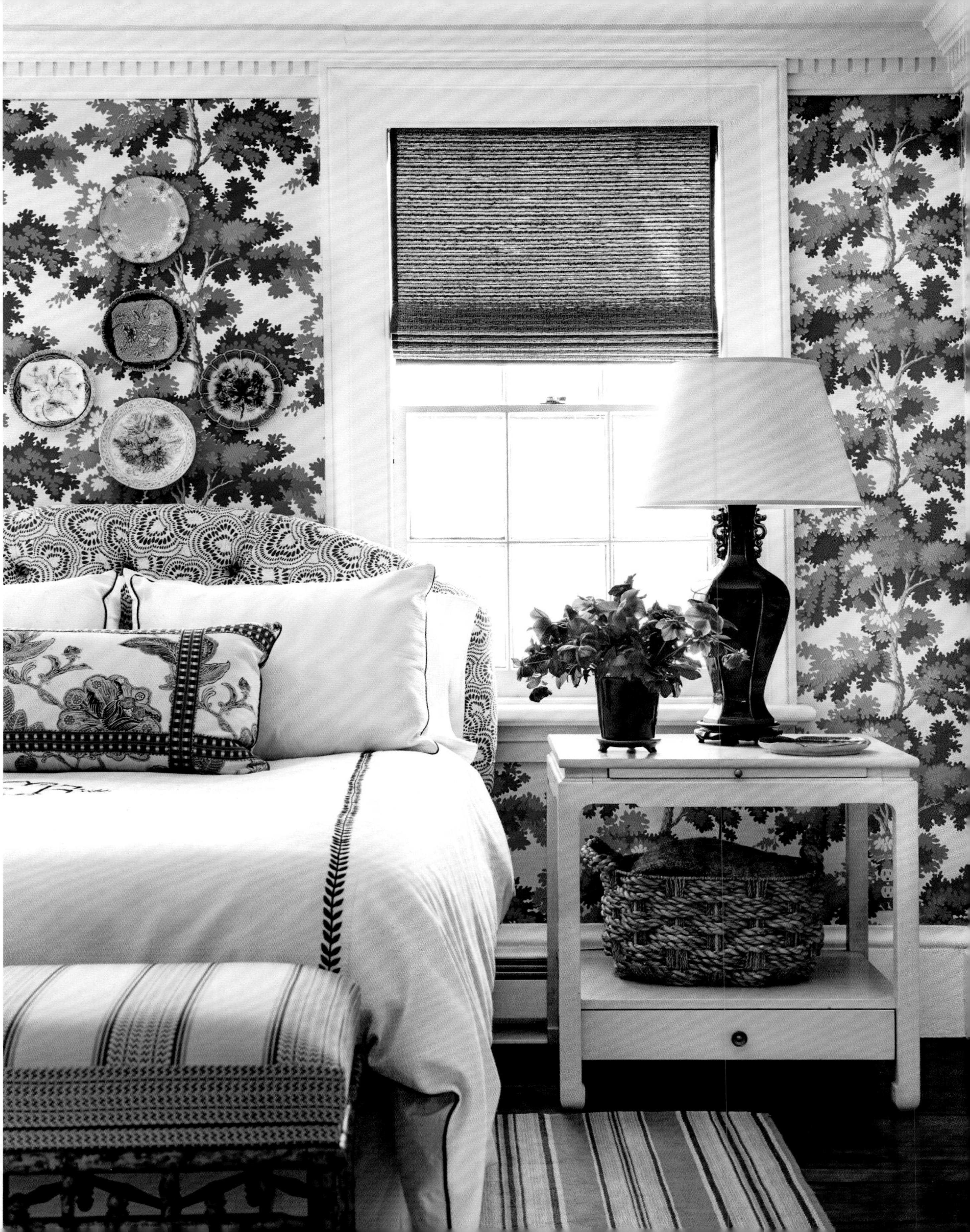

OPPOSITE A mélange of pattern in a master bedroom starts with the enchanted forest on the walls. Woodland wallpaper mixes with a headboard pattern reminiscent of the concentric rings inside a tree trunk.

THIS PAGE Fanciful abstract branches stenciled over grass cloth lend a grounding effect to a master bedroom to warm the sky-high ceiling.

AN ALFRESCO PARTY HUB

Five stories above Brooklyn, a brownstone's tar-paper roof is transformed into a charming spot for dinner parties—complete with a panoramic view of the skyline.

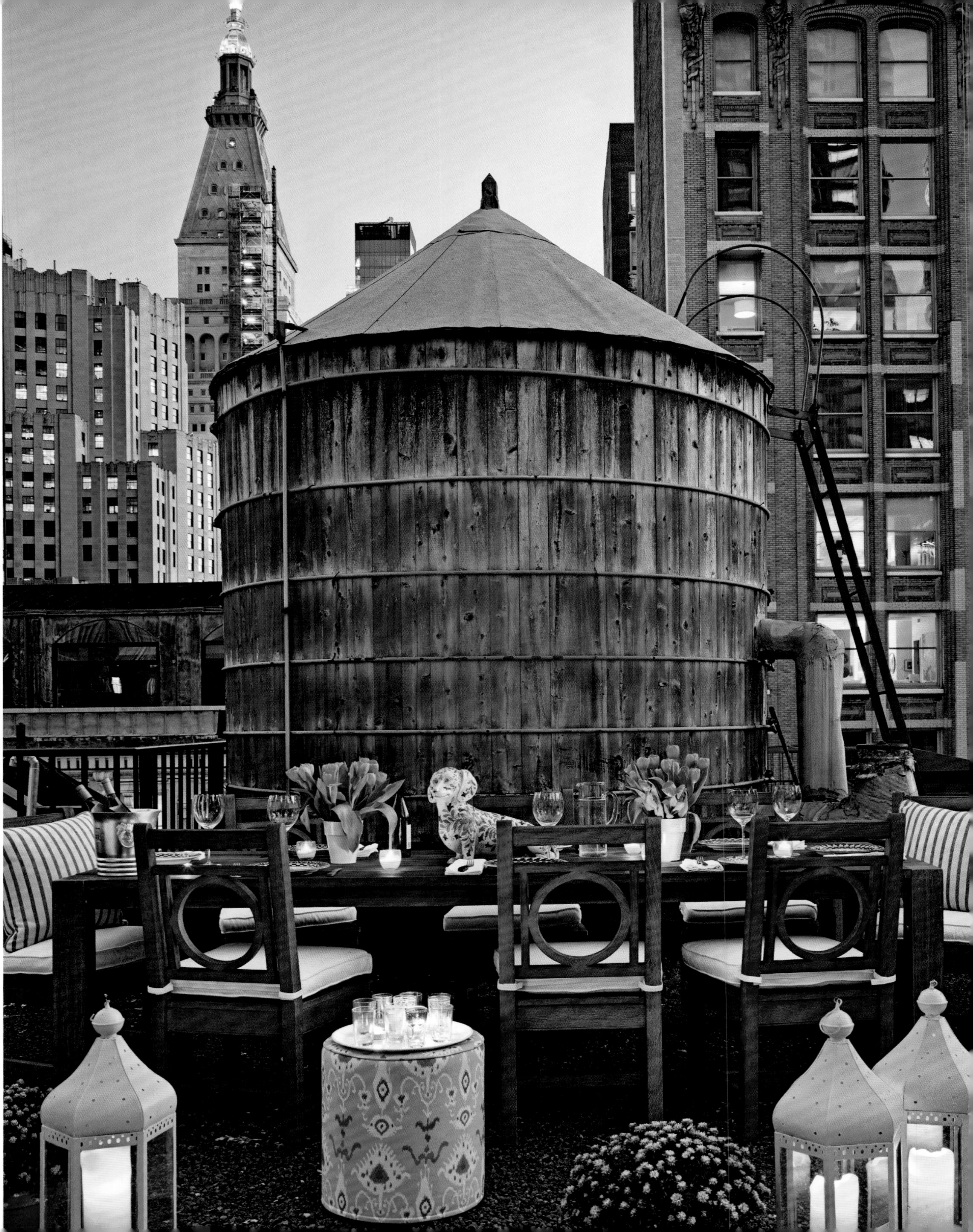

OPPOSITE Tall yellow Moroccan lanterns illuminate a rooftop terrace where a water tank rises above the dinner table like a castle keep.

THIS PAGE String lights suspended over this terrace create the illusion of a ceiling, making the garden feel like a natural extension of the house's first floor.

ILLUSTRATIONS OF birds and beasts have long adorned our most cherished spaces. Why not step outside your species and create your own peaceable kingdom?

A folk art painting of a horse, once featured on the broad side of a barn, was mounted on a track in this office. The owner is a therapist and the massive door slides open to reveal a desk and files that are hidden during sessions.

CLOCKWISE FROM TOP LEFT Tibetan tigers roar from the walls of a wet bar, making parties even more boisterous. Doesn't every serious library need a comical rattan monkey-table? It takes a bold personality to greet visitors to your home with a Korean tiger scroll. Elephants and camels parade across a panoramic wallpaper panel, giving this entry a whiff of the exotic East.

LEFT Channeling the classic English country library on Long Island,, a painting of horses hangs on a traditional knotty-pine-paneled wall. The mohair sofa calls to mind the red-jacketed riders of a foxhunt.

ABOVE Scenic wallpaper made from four English hunting prints—digitized, spliced, and enlarged—creates maximum equine impact in a powder room.

CLOCKWISE FROM TOP LEFT The zebra pattern on dining chairs was designed by the homeowner and executed in needlepoint by her mother. This homeowner's favorite color is navy, and she loves a good zebra print, so in this kitchen she delights in both every day. Even the upholsterer couldn't believe this sofa was destined for an orange animal print, but ivory curtains help soften its brio. A lively turquoise pattern on dining room chairs recalls the rippling sea outside this seaside Florida vacation house.

A ceramic figurine on a coffee table affirms the enduring appeal of the zebra motif in interior design. From the Hollywood Regency style on the West Coast to the late Albert Hadley's iconic love for zebra hooked rugs, the familiar black and white pattern is still the perfect answer when a too-serious room needs a bit of tongue-in-chic.

Deep brown walls give this sofa's verdant Josef Frank-print fabric the appearance of being planted in rich loamy soil—the perfect country house accompaniment.

THIS PAGE The walls and doors of a tiny Manhattan elevator vestibule are sheathed head to toe in huge-scale banana leaves—the print propels visitors out of the tightly confined space into the open loft beyond.

OPPOSITE A vintage bathroom in Cape Cod, like something lifted from the *Thin Man* movies, maintains its Jazz Age elegance even through a refresh. Walls are newly covered in small-scale leaves and there's a rose-strewn slipper chair for towels.

NOT ALL OF us were saddled by Hitchcock with a phobia of birds—many of us find joy in feathering our nests with joyful avian illustrations.

LEFT So many Chinese porcelain birds perched on gold brackets line this Dallas dining room that the room feels like an aviary. A single figurine might have seemed a little "granny," but dozens? The look is more art installation than kitsch.

ABOVE A framed bird print—a very low-maintenance pet—is cheekily hung inside an eye-catching nineteenth-century French birdcage in this bedroom.

CLOCKWISE FROM TOP LEFT A carved Asian lacquer screen shoos a flock of unusual birdlife behind a living room sofa. A sparkling beaded peacock in this San Francisco home office makes bill paying much less onerous. Peacocks swirl around the powder room mirror, giving this Manhattan apartment a taste of life amid the landed gentry. Instead of one print centered over a console, two hung in an asymmetrical stagger are infinitely more interesting.

Like a froth of colored icing topping off a cake, this detail of a pretty bluebird against a pink sky—in artwork by Paule Marrot—makes the heart race a little faster.

CHAPTER VI

EVERY ROOM NEEDS SOMETHING THAT SAYS "TOUCH ME"

• • •

TOUCH IS LITERALLY THE MOST SENSUAL OF SENSES—
DON'T NEGLECT IT. WHETHER UNDERFOOT,
BENEATH YOUR HAND, OR CARESSING YOUR CHEEK,
TEXTURE MAKES A CONNECTION.

OPPOSITE Draped in luxurious downy sheepskins, metal dining chairs are infinitely more inviting than their bare-steel underpinnings would initially suggest. A dynamic espalier-pattern wallpaper with 3-D depth proves even the visual notion of "touch" adds lushness.

TASSELS, FRINGE, NAILHEADS, EVEN FEATHERS!

LOOK CLOSELY—even the smallest of tactile details can make a room overwhelmingly tempting to touch.

OPPOSITE The nailheads fired into the oval backs of these leather dining chairs provide a sensation at once smooth and rough. Pulling out a chair is like stroking a hand-tooled Hermès saddle.

THIS PAGE Three layers of frothy white wool trimming the bottom of a table skirt are the only ornamentation needed in this elegant foyer.

ABOVE Nailhead trim embellishes the fantastical form of this nubby, burlap-covered headboard. Besides being fetchingly touchable, the nailheads provide a strong outline that keeps the wild wallpaper from overwhelming the shape of the bed.

OPPOSITE, CLOCKWISE FROM TOP LEFT The trick to creating these intricate curtains without going overboard is using ivory matte cotton for the trim. Neutrals get a burst of pizzazz from a bed coverlet dotted with large wedding-bell tassels. It's impossible to resist caressing this embossed, peacock-feather wallcovering. A velvet window seat for a lady's office is made extra plush by a brushy fringe that tickles the back of the knees.

TUFTING IS the art of using needle and thread to pull regular indentations into a piece of fabric and batting, leaving behind a pattern of small humps, like moguls on a ski slope. Even master upholsterers find the anchoring and finishing of thread ends a time-consuming challenge, but the comfort is well worth the effort. Tufts sewn in a diamond shape and finished with buttons, like you'd see on a chesterfield sofa, are considered the height of traditional design, but even Modernists have a soft spot for tufting—think Mies van der Rohe and his iconic Barcelona Chair.

Deeply embedded golden tufts and hand-stitched arms that curl up into rams' horns make these chairs indulgent to the eye and pure sybaritic pleasure to sink into.

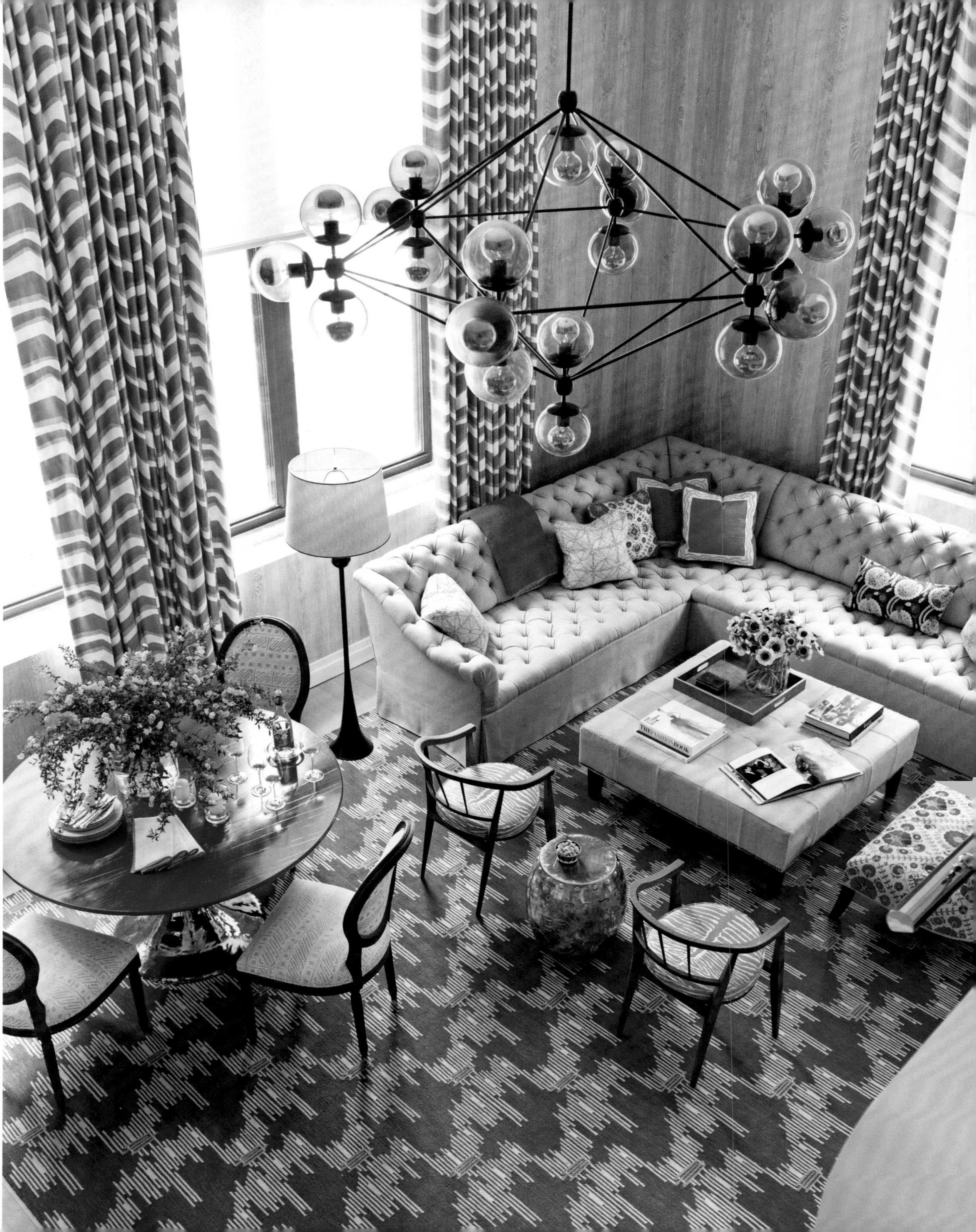
THE FASHION BOOK

OPPOSITE Need something to interrupt an endless expanse of solid fabric? Give thanks for tufting. Pillowy luxury breaks up this large living room sectional with tone-on-tone pattern.

THIS PAGE A round Napoléon III–style settee has a swirling button-tufted elegance in a foyer, creating a place to collapse after shopping or sit patiently waiting for "madame" to descend the stairs.

Button tufts that run all the way to the ceiling convey the ultimate in comfort, especially when surrounded by the walls of curtains that engulf this entire bedroom in misty blue.

CLOCKWISE FROM TOP LEFT What better way to wrap a little girl in sweet dreams than with a pink-tufted wall? Grosgrain ribbon sewn onto this headboard's button tufts looks like daisies and lends a cheery spirit. An undulating tufted headboard transforms a bedroom into a peaceful white cloud. The sumptuousness of tufted mohair on a 1940s Maison Jansen bed contrasts with the room's simple white-plank walls.

WOOD WORN BY TIME

WOOD WORN smooth by the march of years and the touch of countless passersby invites your hand as well.

OPPOSITE The front doors of this home were crafted from 1850s Italian oak. Reclaimed wood, sourced from an antiquities dealer, is what gives this newly built home its soulful character.

THIS PAGE Ten-foot-tall French wood shutters were retrofitted to the dimensions of a window and installed on a metal track so they'd open and close like curtains.

THIS PAGE A casual dining area is dominated by a mammoth live-edge Provençal table made from an old timber slab that's grown gloriously wavy with wear.

OPPOSITE This living room's clear cypress walls were stained dark and washed with a lichen-color glaze. The ceiling is pecky cypress for contrast and the stain on the floor introduces green and gray tones for a cool feel. The carefully chosen finishes create a harmonious atmosphere and a whispery sense of calm.

THIS PAGE A rough and faded nineteenth-century French apothecary case (cheaper to install than new upper cabinets!) anchors this kitchen and gives it instant character. For contrast, the owner chose a sleek modern island encased in Carrara marble.

OPPOSITE This kitchen cabinet's highly distressed louvered doors are actually new. They were custom made, then painted, stripped, and chipped to make a lyrical foil for all the stainless steel and marble.

IN THE EARLY 1800s new looms mechanized the time-consuming process of making velvet, and suddenly the luxurious cloth of kings and cardinals was affordable to a broader, if still well-heeled, clientele. At its most basic, velvet is a densely looped pile, originally silk, with the loops then cut to create a plush "hand" that reflects light and is incredibly soft to the touch. Over the centuries, craftsmen learned to vary the height and color of the pile to build pattern and could brocade the cloth with precious materials, like gold and silver threads worthy of their royal clientele. Early velvet production occurred only in historic luxury hubs like Baghdad, Timbuktu, Venice, and Bruges. But today velvet can be made from a variety of affordable materials, even synthetics, making its rippling sheen and lush texture available to all.

. . . .

The sectional sofa in this library got a full dose of ultramarine velvet. Besides adding vibrancy to an otherwise traditional library, the sofa is so comfortable it's become the spot where the homeowners crash after a long day.

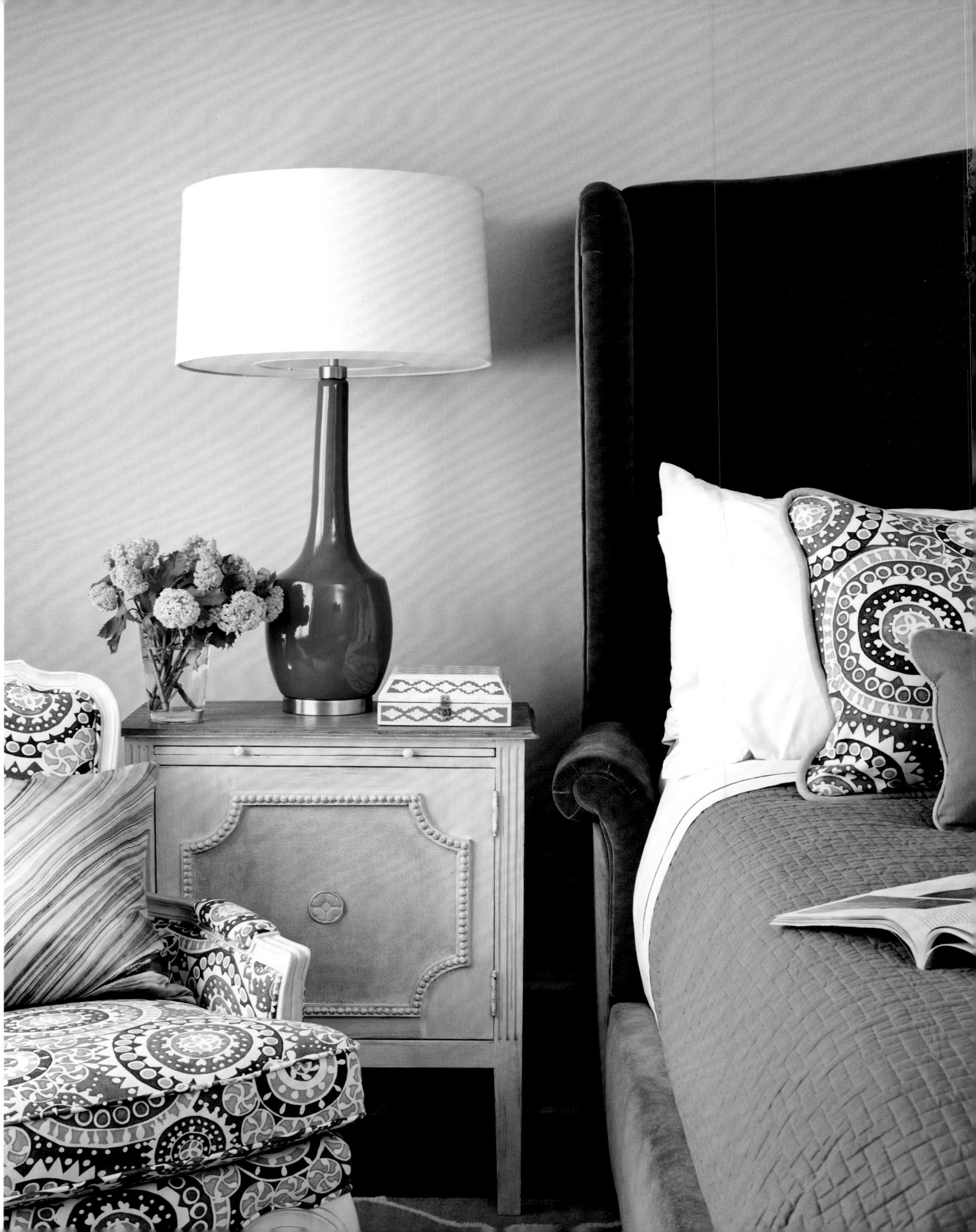

OPPOSITE Talk about being treated royally! Could anything feel cozier than flopping down on a regal velvet bed? It gives a recently built home the kind of warmth that's hard to instill in new construction.

THIS PAGE For a completely over-the-top and unexpected touch, the mirrors flanking this fireplace are framed in olive velvet, complementing an oversized Moorish-style ottoman covered in a swath of velvet so striking the family calls the piece "the jolly green giant!"

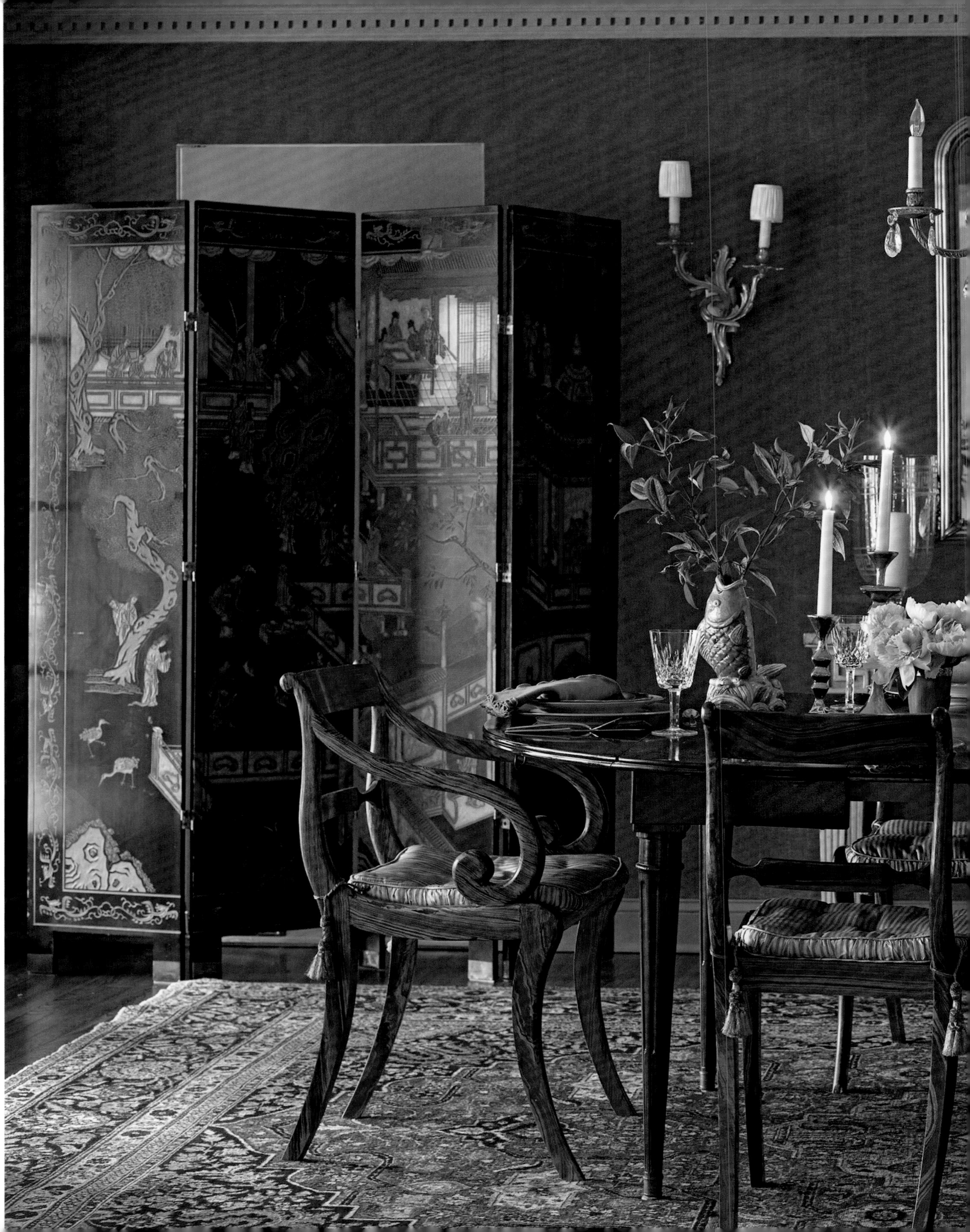

For walls as verdant as a summer woodland, this dining room was sheathed in forest-green velvet. The room has more depth than paint could ever provide, and the fabric has a luster that literally glows in candlelight. Visitors invariably do a double-take and reach out to stroke the walls.

THE RAW MATERIALS used to make a grass cloth wallcovering—jute, sisal, hemp, and reeds—are not prone to perfection and therein lies their beauty. Held together with cotton thread or sea grass, then fastened to rice paper backing, grass cloth can be rough or shiny, colorful or neutral, light or dark—but never boring. There's no more impactful way to celebrate nature (and texture) in a home.

The sheen of fibers in the persimmon-colored grass cloth in this entry adds a touch of sparkle to welcome guests. Walls that say "please touch" make the imposing Park Avenue duplex more approachable.

The oatmeal-colored grass cloth below the chair rail lends youth to the hand-tooled aqua and bronze fantasy above, so this dining room fends off the baroque and embraces conviviality.

CLOCKWISE FROM TOP LEFT Lemony grass cloth draws the eye to a modern glass ceiling fixture in this apartment entry. The intense shade of tropical green on these breakfast room walls is softened by the light-absorbing quality of grass cloth. Climbing a narrow stairway surrounded by textural walls feels like winding your way up a spiraling castle turret. When there are four young children romping around a family room, durability is key, and navy raffia walls are practically bulletproof.

CHAPTER VII

EVERY ROOM NEEDS SOMETHING THAT SPEAKS ONLY TO *YOU*

• • •

WHY CAN'T IT BE ALL ABOUT YOU? *WHEN IT COMES TIME TO TIE A BOW AROUND YOUR HOME DÉCOR, MAKE SURE TO INCLUDE A GIFT TO SELF.* WHETHER IT'S A WALL OF FAMILY PHOTOS, MEMENTOS FROM VACATIONS PAST, OR SOME ESPECIALLY CHERISHED HEIRLOOM, YOU CAN CREATE A SPACE THAT BRINGS YOU JOY.

OPPOSITE A stylist's home office is his room for dreaming. Shelves serve as an inspiration board and revolving groups of objects, collected for no reason other than that the owner finds them beautiful, are regularly arranged and rearranged. He leans back in his Jacobsen Swan chair, gazes at his shelves, and lets inspiration come.

THINGS THAT MAKE YOU HAPPY,
ON DISPLAY, EVERY DAY

OPPOSITE Originally a vessel for storing precious spices, Chinese ginger jars are today the focus of obsession for collectors. These blue-and-white beauties (antique or not!) provide punch when grouped together. Passing by a massed host of them is the path to visual joy.

THIS PAGE Who would have guessed tart, apple-green lacquer would be the perfect offset to such an eclectic assemblage? The tangy color highlights the owner's collections (high and low) of coral, shells, and porcelains. Each object further beautifies the next.

In his bedroom, this homeowner placed a quirky stand on a marble-topped dresser and filled it with red and green tartanware. The plaids pick up the colors of the Alexander Liberman gouache leaning casually against the wall.

CLOCKWISE FROM TOP LEFT After discovering a rustic wood wall hidden behind neon-green drywall in her 1920s house, this homeowner turned it into an inspiration board. Disparate favorites are arranged prettily by a bedside: malachite, perfume, and that indispensable fashion accessory—a leopard turban. The vintage gilt frame over a desk is fitted with corkboard and covered in leftover wallpaper for pinning invitations and keepsakes. In a bookcase niche, porcelain urns match the elegance of a Richard Avedon photograph of the owner's sister.

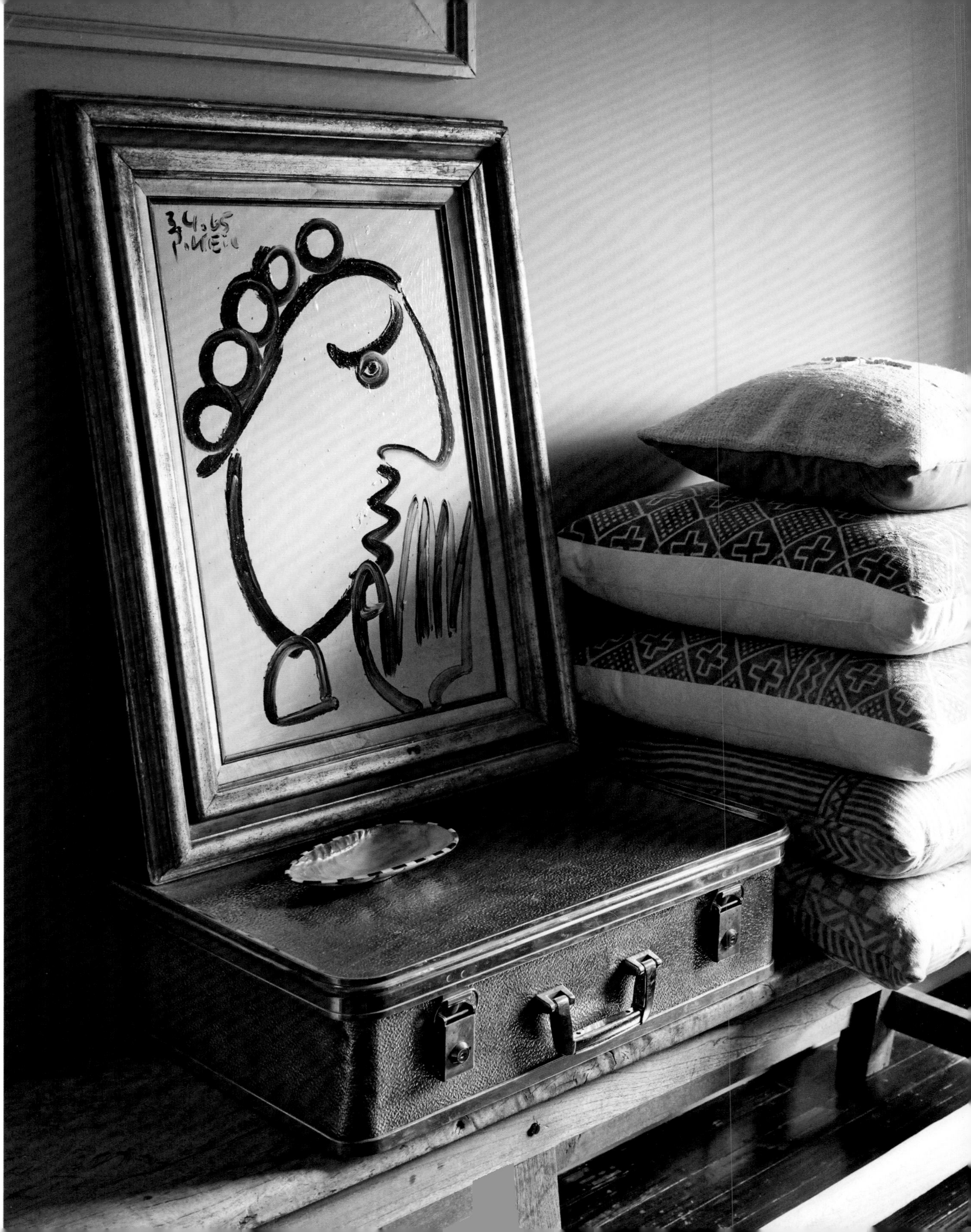

OPPOSITE In a guest room, an abstract circa-1965 portrait resting on a vintage aluminum suitcase creates an oddly beautiful vignette for visitors to enjoy.

THIS PAGE This homeowner discovered Harkerware on eBay, fell in love, and started hanging it on her dining room walls. Covering the entire wall in plates evokes the same effect as one enormous, eye-catching work of art.

ONCE THE Neanderthals mastered bison, bulls, and bears for their cave décor, portraits were probably the next artistic effort in line. The Egyptians, Greeks, and Romans all went in for portraiture, often as funerary recognition of a great man's passing, while the artists of the Italian Renaissance produced fantastic works like Da Vinci's *Mona Lisa*, but weren't above idealizing the features of a homely Medici or two. In the Netherlands, the plainspoken Dutch brought middle-class subjects and painfully accurate representation to the field, and then, in the eighteenth and nineteenth centuries, the British opened the floodgates, with every minor viscount and baronet competing for the talent of masters like Thomas Gainsborough and an interloping American named John Singer Sargent.

. . . .

Portraits are hung floor to ceiling like three-dimensional wallpaper. The owner has been collecting them for forty-five years and can tell a tale of provenance and subject for each and every piece. He says just looking at his wall triggers fond memories of the hunt.

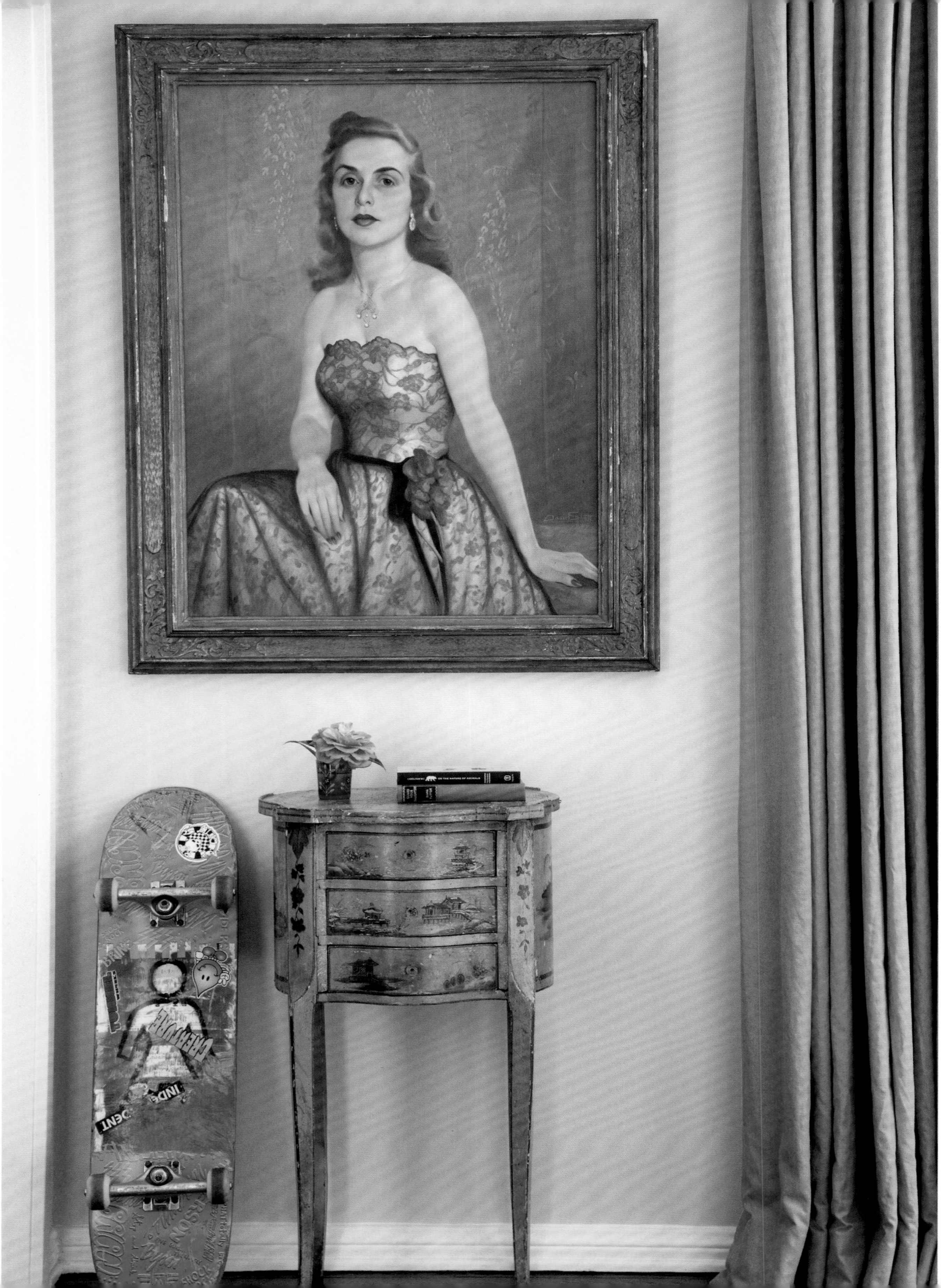

OPPOSITE A portrait of the homeowner's mother hangs above her son's skateboard and an heirloom table to form a multi-generational collage. By surrounding themselves with touchstones that have real meaning, this family has given their home uncommon warmth.

THIS PAGE The new owners of a 1850s country house bought this portrait of a soldier from the previous owners—they didn't want to throw him out of his house! Hung on such high-spirited wallpaper, he's been reenlisted in an entirely new life.

CLOCKWISE FROM TOP LEFT A small painting of the homeowner as a child feels almost like it's on a pedestal, hung above an oversized antique urn. A homeowner with a soft spot for canines fills an upstairs hallway with what else? Dog portraits. Four fanciful prints of courtly gentlemen on a swirling cloud of wallpaper lend the feel of a grisaille mural. A painting of an unknown gentleman found in an antiques store oversees a dining room; the owners refer to him jocularly as Great-Uncle Charles.

Ancestral portraits bring a sense of history to a family's Vermont weekend house. Black frames play off red lacquered walls and brighten the personalities of the portraits' rather dour subjects.

This playroom will not be outgrown. Today, it perfectly suits its five- and seven-year-old denizens. But once the kids reach their teens, the colorful space will convert to a fabulous lacquered-green lounge.

OPPOSITE Punchy pattern and lively hues turned a previously stiff and formal paneled library in a white-glove Park Avenue building into a kid- (and dog-) friendly playroom.

THIS PAGE This children's reading nook is a niche carved from an upstairs hallway. Drawing the curtains turns it into a magical secret compartment where pint-sized imaginations can run wild.

A boat chandelier and framed maritime flag reflect the nautical theme in this boy's bedroom that doubles as playroom in a small Manhattan apartment. The low table is a play surface with toy storage underneath, while a banquette by the window provides a comfortable spot for adult supervision.

CLOCKWISE FROM TOP LEFT Custom stairs make it a snap to reach the top berth in this girls' bunkroom in a mountain chalet. A mural in a children's bedroom transforms the ceiling into a canopy of trees and sky. Vibrant wallpaper energizes a boys' bathroom where rubber duckies toddle across the windowsill. A teenagers' billiards room has a lively vibe with its exotic hanging lantern.

A WORKSTATION

MANY PEOPLE find they're more productive at home than schmoozing with the gang at the company water cooler. And so the door has been flung wide open to a new opportunity for interior design—welcome, the chic home office.

. . . .

Texture is used to great effect in a black-and-white home office where a straw pendant light illuminates zebra-print chairs found in a French flea market. The space says: "Creative work is in progress."

CLOCKWISE FROM TOP LEFT It feels somehow simultaneously lively and peaceful in a room where a minimal desk pairs with a bright yellow dhurrie rug. In a designer's personal lair, a vaguely Moorish wall stencil frames a chinoiserie chest and a Parsons table made sleek by auto paint. The desk in this home is perfectly placed to receive the luminous light reflecting in from the landscape. A floating desk and acrylic chair keep bulky legs to a minimum in a tight space.

A PLACE TO NESTLE IN

CALL IT NESTING, burrowing, or just getting cozy, mankind does have a primal need for a den—a place to sink in and feel safe and relaxed and, for just a few minutes, sheltered from the worries of the world.

. . . .

Even without that big fire blazing in the background, this daybed would radiate warmth.

CLOCKWISE FROM TOP LEFT Light from a pierced brass lantern dapples a woman's upstairs hideout for a magical effect. Having a built-in bed in a beach house home office means living with the ever-present temptation of an afternoon nap. A previously unused niche is transformed into a much-loved reading nook by a cushy daybed and oversized pillows. There's no better spot to enjoy the San Francisco sunsets than sprawled on this improvised hammock made from rope, wood, and metal rings.

All it took to create a cozy corner in a guest room was an antique bench with a soft cushion and a place to rest a cup of tea.

OPPOSITE The firebox inside this intricately patterned Moroccan tile fireplace was built high above the floor so the homeowners can watch the flickering embers from the comfort of their bed.

THIS PAGE A replica of a sixteenth-century Italian mantel depicting a ravenous, grinning, wart-nosed monster turned this postage-stamp-sized fireplace into a phantasmagorical focal point.

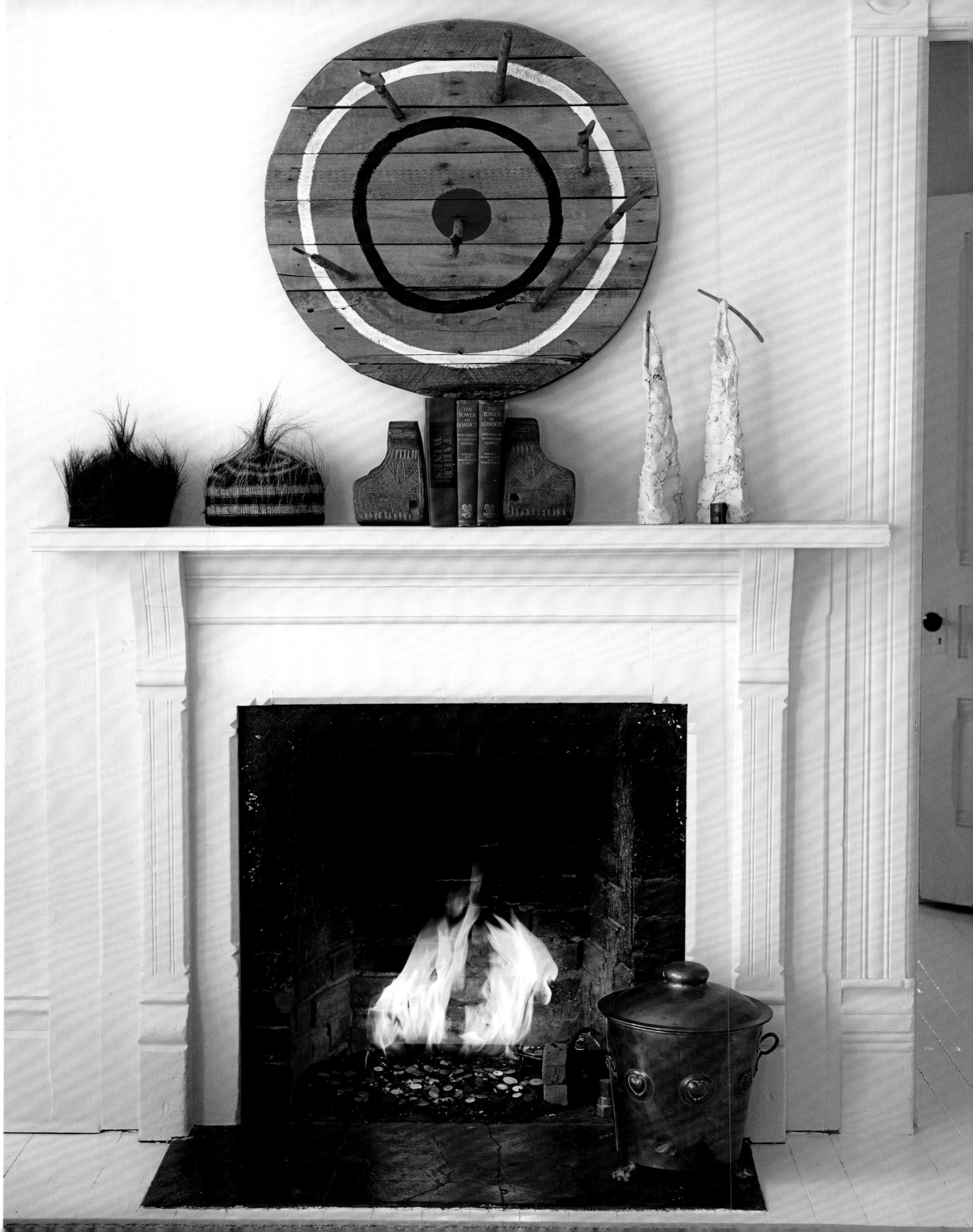

{A HEARTH SURE TO START A FIRESIDE CHAT}

OPPOSITE Whenever he returns from abroad, this owner throws his foreign pocket change into the fireplace. The coins reflect the dancing flames and evoke memories of his far-flung travels.

THIS PAGE The designer of this charming guest room loves to tell about a grand house he once knew where a butler would lay the wood for a fire, then leave behind a decorative newspaper fan so it would light easily with a single match. The fan here is an inside joke; the logs are electric!

FOR HUNDREDS of years, medieval lords lived with smoking, spitting cook fires at the center of their great halls until some bright twelfth-century architect had the inspiration to move the fireplace to an exterior wall. Innovations like chimneys and flues soon followed, and before long the hearth had become an integral part of every home—and one more décor opportunity. The mantel—originally a hood that projected out over the fire to capture smoke—was reimagined in marble and limestone by Renaissance craftsmen, carved in fine woods by the Scottish Adam brothers, and even sculpted from stone by the great Augustus Saint-Gaudens. Today's houses may not need open cook fires, but that hasn't diminished the importance of the hearth as the warm, beating heart of the home.

A massive free-standing brick fireplace cuts through three stories of this house—from the basement below, to this light-filled living room, and up to a roof deck. Finished in jet black, the hearth dominates the room like an important piece of sculpture.

A FAMILY PORCH

THE BEST FAMILY porches are like the best potato salads— nothing fancy, nothing extra, but perfect in every way.

On a sparkling Down East day, true Mainers want to be outdoors, and a screened porch overlooking the harbor is everyone's first choice for a family meal. Chairs and table are made of indestructible all-weather aluminum with a glossy white finish so they can, quite literally, be hosed down.

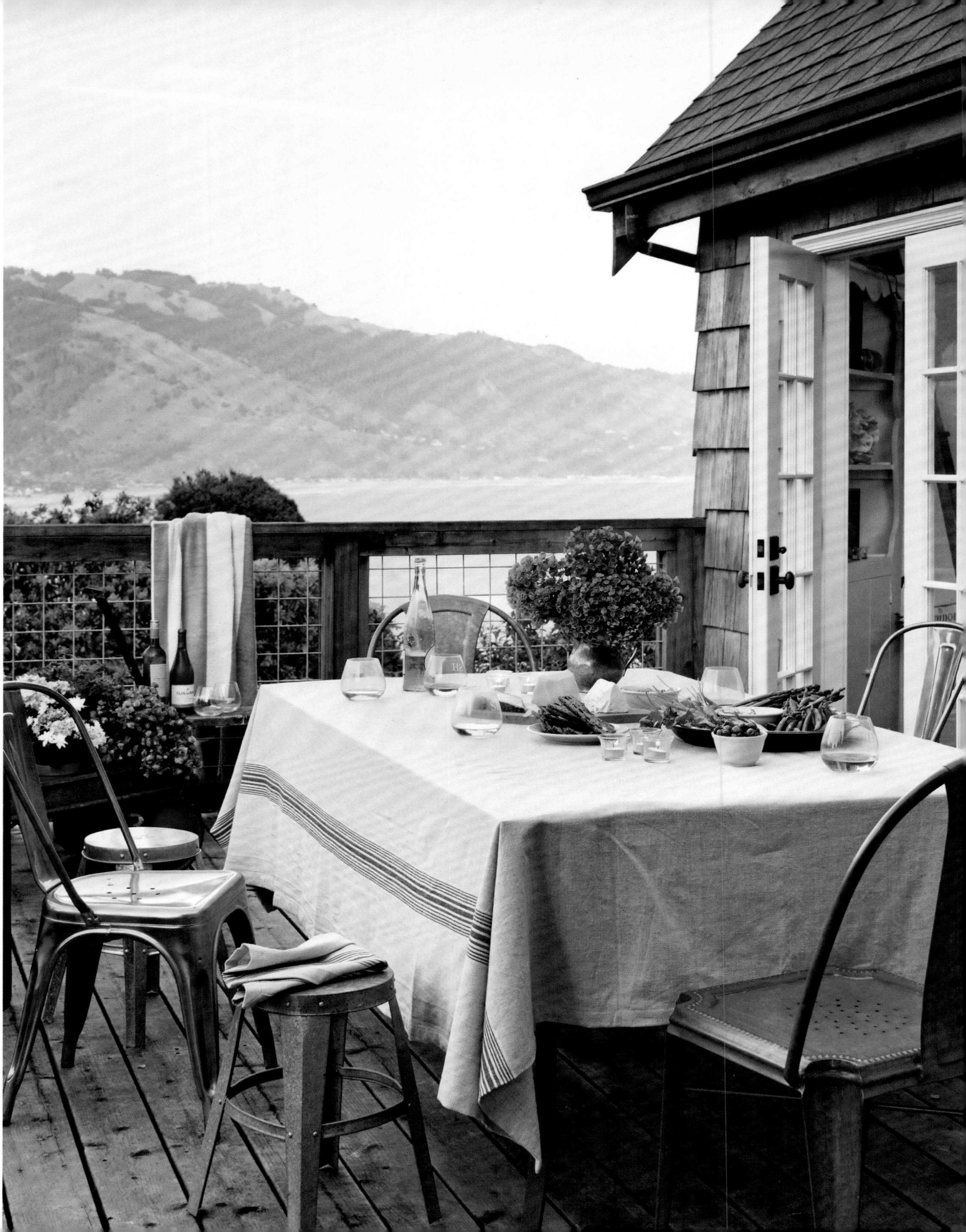

OPPOSITE At a getaway house in the rugged hills of Marin County, California, everything about the outdoor dining area is kept simple. An assortment of galvanized metal furniture surrounds a table draped with a homespun cloth of washable cotton and linen.

THIS PAGE With a rock collection lining its railings and tree stumps for seats, this Long Island deck is a young family's low-key paradise. The table and bench are made of cedar planking salvaged from old Manhattan water towers. The owner designed and rigged the homemade roof of lashed bamboo poles.

CHAPTER VIII

EVERY ROOM NEEDS A "WOW" MOMENT

• • •

FAINT HEART NE'ER WON FAIR LADY, SO GO AHEAD AND SHOCK 'EM. DO YOU WANT TO BE THE STAR OF THE SHOW OR THE UNDERSTUDY? TAKE A RISK.

OPPOSITE Eight striking etchings by Anish Kapoor seem to pulse with inner light. An entire wall of them makes a strong visual statement on its own, but to underscore the drama by matching all the colors in the room to the art's neon hues is simply audacious.

THIS PAGE An antique bust gives visitors the once-over at this Manhattan studio apartment entry, adding a note of classical opulence that belies the place's modest square footage.

OPPOSITE The ancient Roman goddess Juno rules over all she surveys from atop her plinth in this pint-sized dining room in a 1907 cottage. Collected in France, the monumental plaster cast is a brave choice for a diminutive space.

In a master bedroom, a papier-mâché buck's head nods hello from an autumnal field of chocolate-brown grass cloth.

CLOCKWISE FROM TOP LEFT In this Rhode Island beach house a niche features a bronze of Sassacus, chief of the Pequots when the tribe held dominion over the southern New England coast. A Greek gentleman seems a trifle surprised at sharing his bookcase with an alabaster octopus. A sculpted horsehead in the window might conjure up memories of Mister Ed for bathers of a certain age. This stone bust of a woman seems a much better choice than a jewelry box to display necklaces.

LIPSTICK RED

OLD HOLLYWOOD makeup artists knew their stuff. If it's star power you want, try a slash of scarlet across the lips.

OPPOSITE Talk about a fiery personality: There's nothing shy about this flame-stitched velvet wallcovering. But if you're game to try it, the color is as heavenly in bright sunshine as on a gray dreary day.

THIS PAGE An intense claret-red leather chair channels the anticipation of that first sip of good red wine on a cold winter's night.

THIS PAGE This blazing velvet sofa alone would knock visitors off their feet, but scarlet curtains and lamps go on to escalate the effect! Not for the timid.

OPPOSITE Red looks even redder in a glossy coat of crimson lacquer. Placed against library walls covered in cobalt wool, this secretary is proof that a single piece of furniture in a boldly chosen color can change a room from staid to dazzling.

The owner's handiwork—Japanese sumi-e ink drawings on antique paper—fills a wall above a living room banquette. In this ancient art, careful thought goes into each stroke of the intense jet-black ink. Grouped together, the paintings have stunning graphic presence.

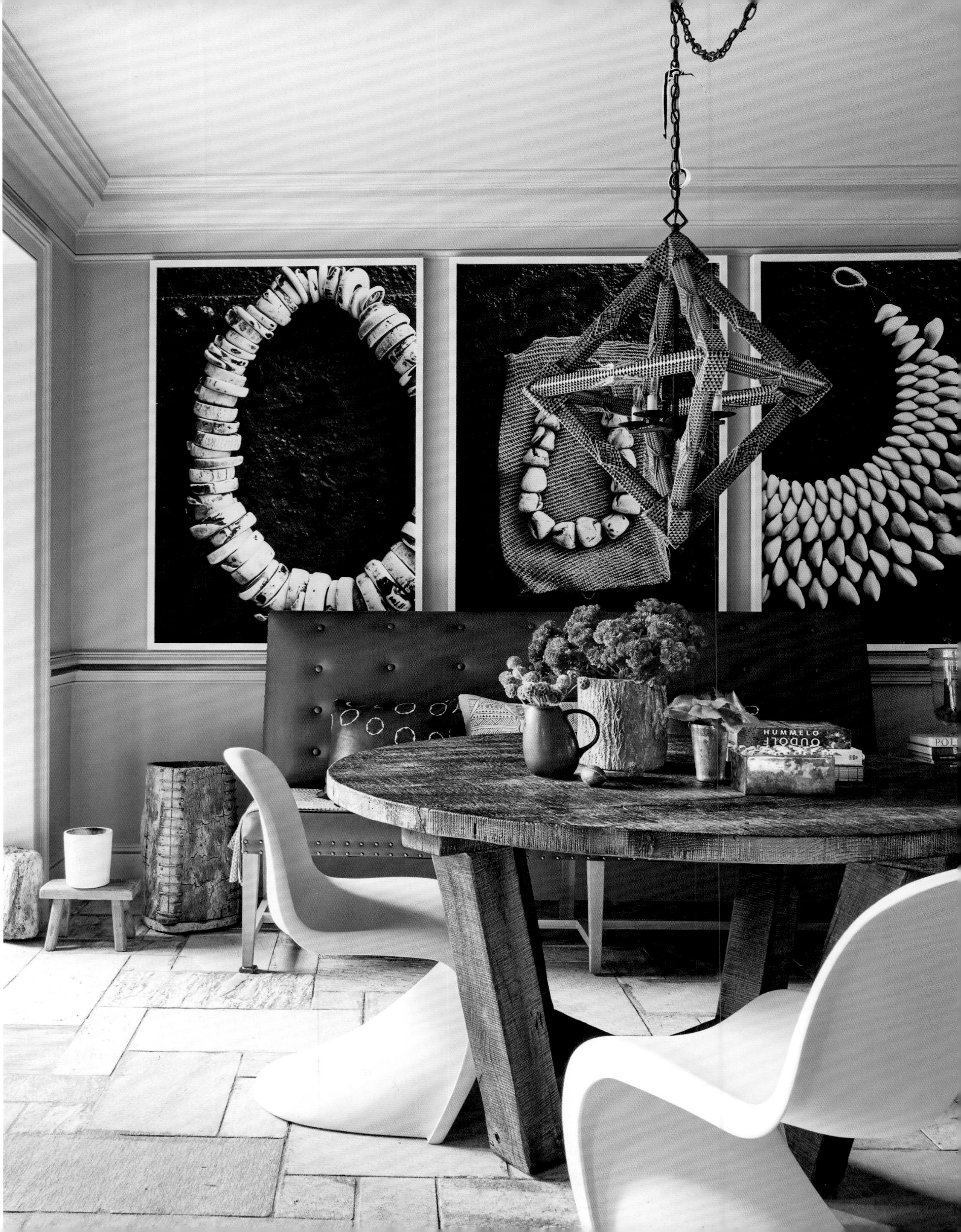
HUMMELO

OPPOSITE Gutsy and intriguing, Rob Brinson's overscaled photographs of tribal jewelry have a mystical hold on this room. The low ceiling and shadowy palette make it seem as if you're dining in a clandestine underground chamber.

THIS PAGE Don't be fooled by these baroque moldings and ceiling rosettes in this 18th-century home. An artist embellished this tiny space with chalk. Accidentally brushing up against it is just part of the fun.

THIS PAGE It really doesn't matter what you're serving when you've got cabinetry as glamorous as these gleaming, ebony-lacquered beauties. Nickel hardware adds to the pre-war mystique in a vintage New York apartment.

OPPOSITE Imagine this room trimmed in white instead of black—an entirely different mood, right? The ebony moldings and stripes on the floor lend gravitas to a small Chicago kitchen that doubles as tasting room for the owner, a serious wine connoisseur.

Dark and sexy, this kitchen was built for entertaining or maybe sipping a cocktail while preparing a meal. The dramatic herringbone backsplash is made from alternating matte-black and opalescent glass tiles. When the light is just right, it turns to silver.

IN THE EARLY 1600s the British East India Company and its Dutch, French, and Swedish counterparts began importing tea and spices from the Chinese (*les Chinois* in French). The wealthy, of course, couldn't serve their precious tea in just any old cup, leading to a craze for fine Chinese porcelains, followed soon after by Chinese lacquered furniture, Chinese art, and eventually, all manner of things Chinese. The example set by royal collectors like Louis XV inspired a broader market for this *chinoiserie* and opportunistic European craftsmen began manufacturing domestic copies. As the fashionable crowd moved on to the more restrained classicism of the Louis Seize period, the fad petered out, only to be revived again by the Victorians, most notably at the Brighton Pavilion. In the 1920s and '30s designers found chinoiserie wallpapers, porcelains, and lacquer a perfect match for Art Deco and it has not been out of style since!

In the foyer of a 1930s house, smashing chinoiserie wallpaper (flowers and birds on acid green!) envelops this curved stair-hall like a flamboyant gift wrap.

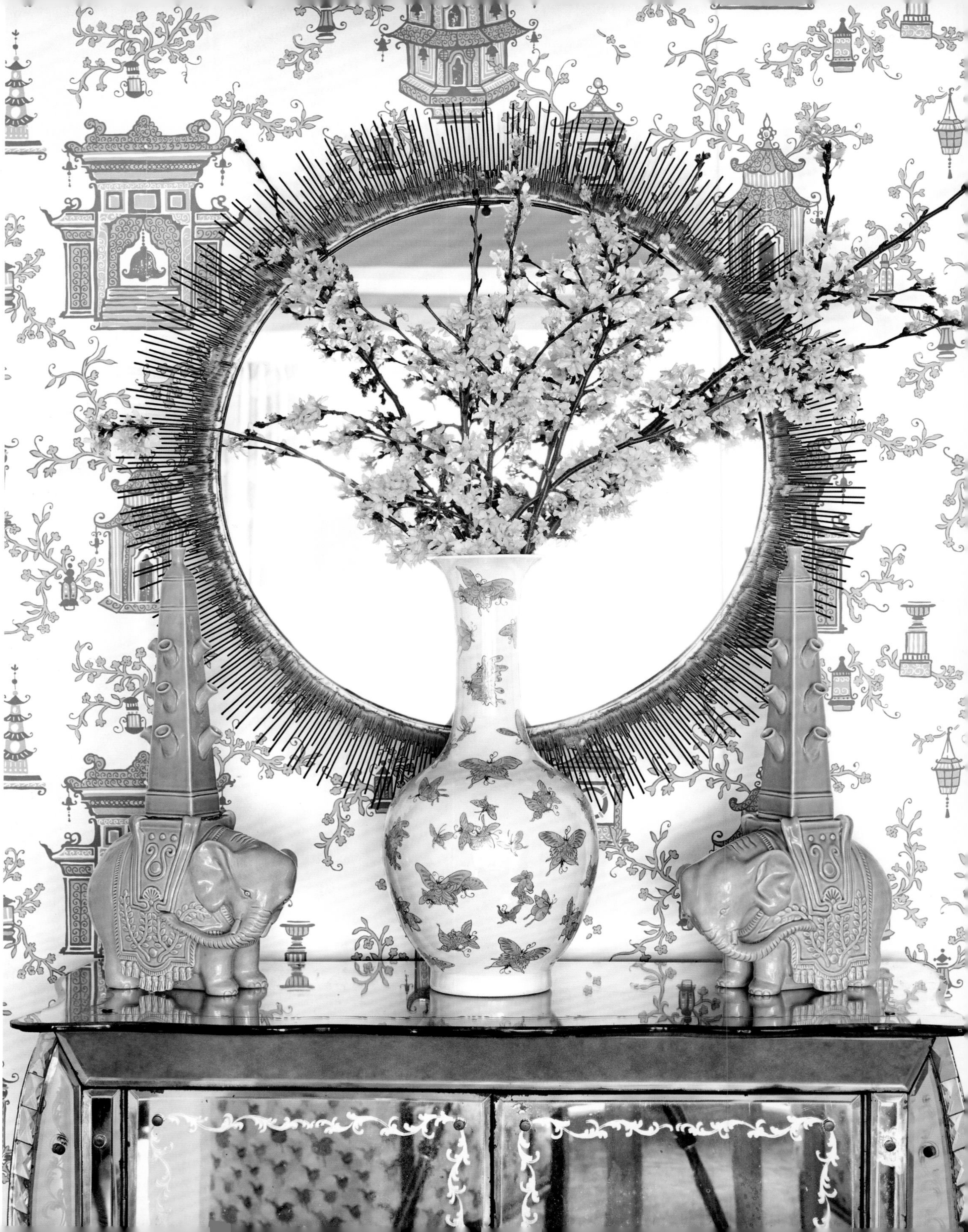

OPPOSITE When you walk into this New York apartment, the entry wallpaper transports you to a far-off place where Chinese pagodas dot the landscape amid trees hung with twinkling lanterns. Two bright-yellow elephant tulipieres complete the sense of escape from the bustling city streets below.

THIS PAGE When you're so infatuated with chinoiserie you can't ever be without it, you cover your headboard, bedskirt, and bench in fabric with East Asian appeal—and fall asleep to dreams of the enchanted East.

CLOCKWISE FROM TOP LEFT A bold lacquer table and contemporary chairs contrast with delicate hand-painted wallpaper. This faux-bamboo, pagoda-shaped mirror painted devil-may-care turquoise, says, "I don't take my Louis XVI furniture seriously, so neither should you!" Chinoiserie wallpaper creates an Asian garden in an apartment in the heart of New York City. A zingy bamboo-print wallpaper in a powder room is a perfect match for the yellow silk shade embellished with pagoda tassels.

A four-foot-high decorative pagoda in a dining room corner gets people talking while breaking down the formality of the silver-leaf wallpaper.

THE PINK CITY: In 1876, while under the rule of the British Raj, Jaipur was visited by the prince of Wales, the future Edward VII, and in a fit of exuberance at this honor, the entire city was painted pink! To this day, broad swathes of the city remain a sun-faded rose that's made its own distinctive contribution to the color wheel.

As an antidote to the gray, foggy days of San Francisco, pink was used with abandon in this living room. Ironically, despite the home's perch in Pacific Heights, the mix of blush and coppery tones was inspired by colors in the sky at sunset on a beach in Maine.

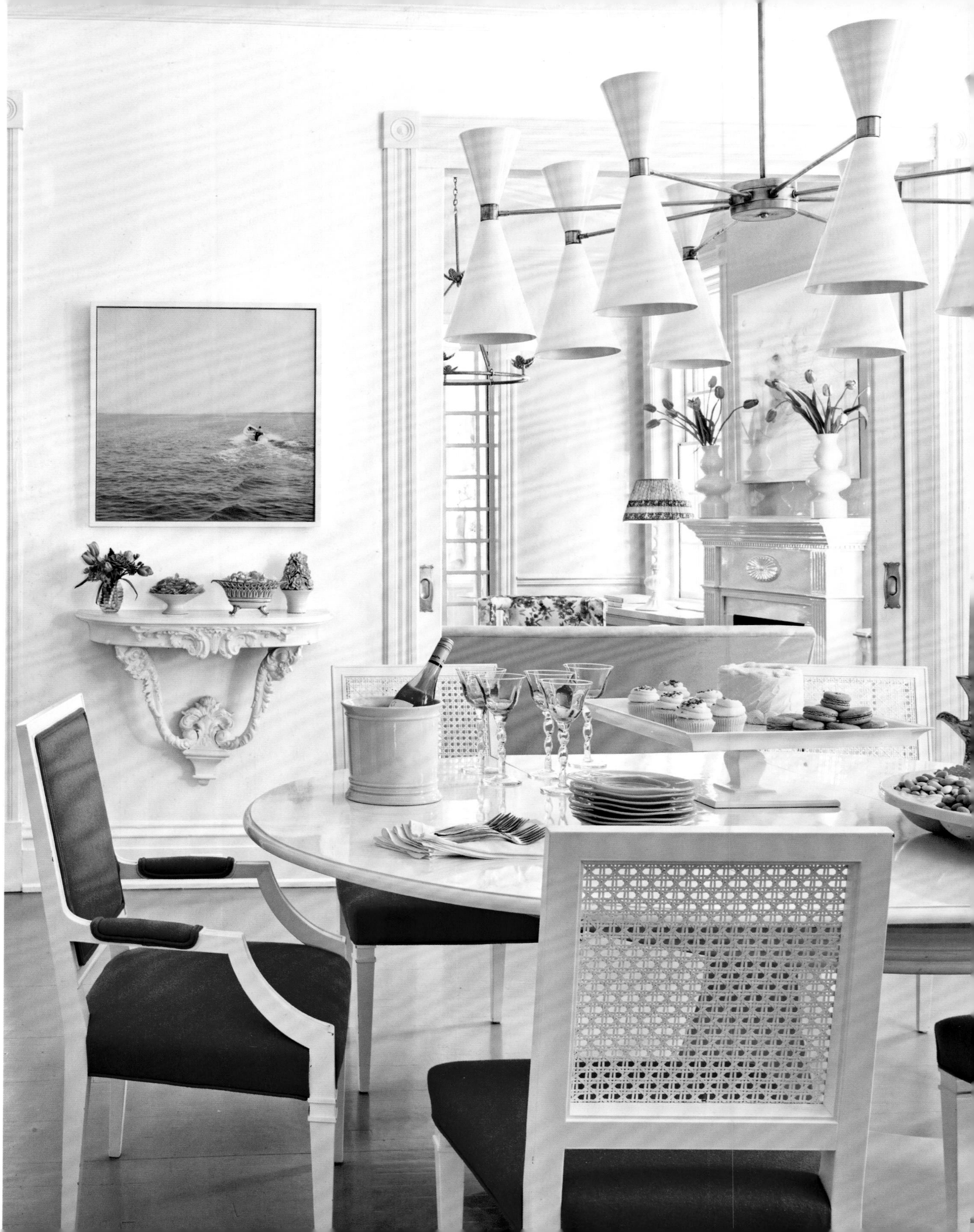

OPPOSITE This dining room's vintage chairs are lacquered white for maximum eye-candy contrast with their vibrant fuchsia seats.

THIS PAGE Warmth so radiates from the walls of this study that just standing in front of them brings a flush to the face. This tone finds a natural complement in blue, so this eye-popping art has even greater impact against its bold background.

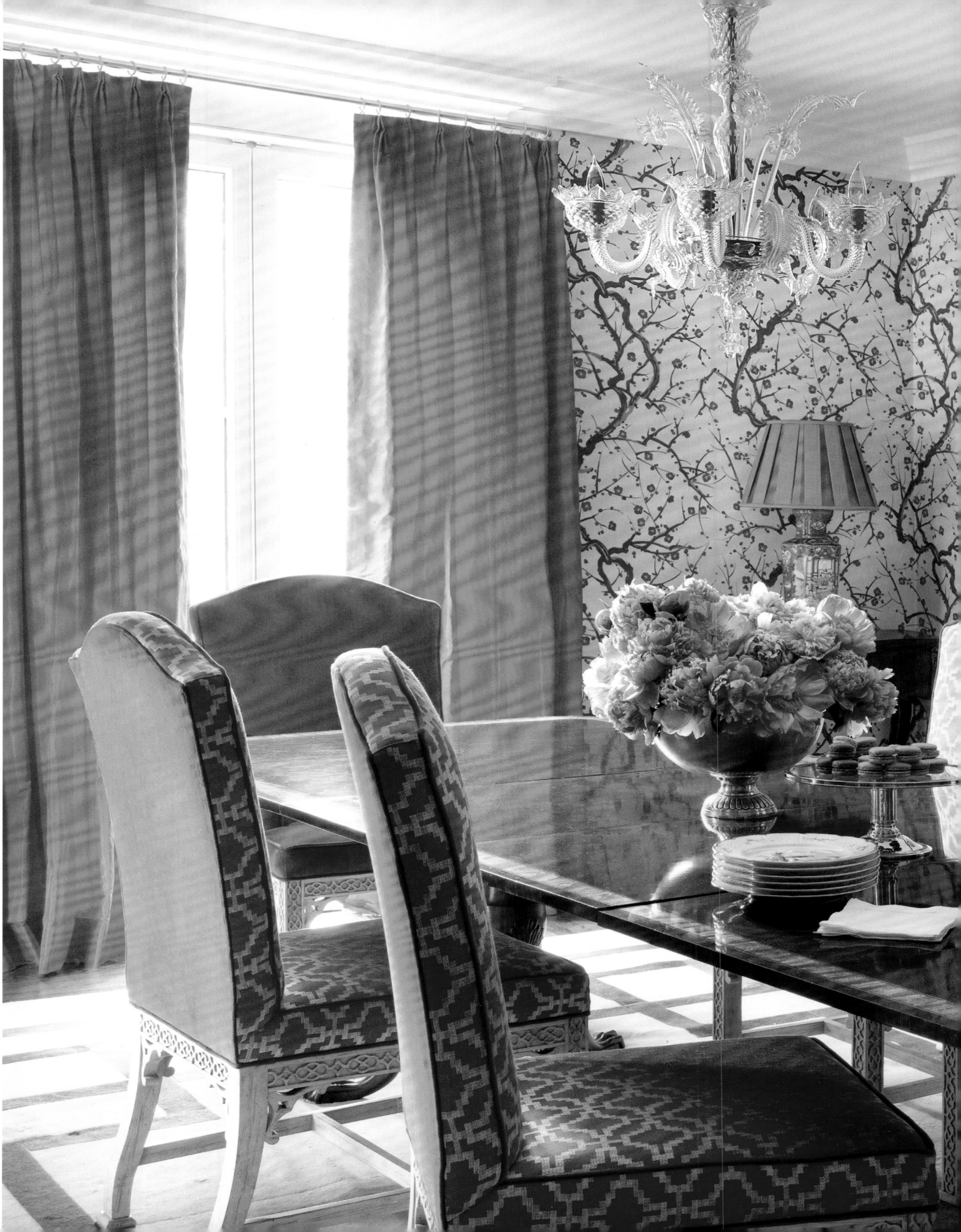

There's nothing demure about setting these dazzling pink dining room curtains against flowering quince wallpaper! In candlelight the silk curtains cast a magical glow on dinner guests that, not coincidentally, is incredibly flattering.

A ROOM ENFOLDED IN FABRIC

Blush tones fold you in a peaceful embrace in this bedroom where the walls and headboard are upholstered in a fantasy woodland— as seen through rose-colored glasses. It's the very embodiment of "sleep tight."

OPPOSITE A daughter's bedroom is a lavishly girly cocoon thanks to its exotic paisley fabric. It's princess of the Raj meets modern preteen.

THIS PAGE Striped fabric completely envelops a bedroom inspired by a famous tented room at the Charlottenhof Palace in Germany. A curtain hung on a red rod at the bedside masks storage. Bright-colored trim lines the room and an old drum made into a chandelier insists you look up and marvel.

Determined to bring a buoyant atmosphere to this living room, the designer selected a vivacious shade of yellow and ran with it. The lantern is outlined in yellow too, so not even nightfall interrupts this room's sunny attitude.

Lemon-yellow chinoiserie wallpaper, white Chippendale-style chairs, and a black painted floor bring touches of Hollywood glamour to this young family's kitchen.

CLOCKWISE FROM TOP LEFT The shock of yellow walls and an even brighter citron table jolt a gray and white kitchen to life. Rich and brilliant high-gloss yellow paint plays "Here Comes the Sun" at daybreak in this master bedroom. Simply dressing the bed in daffodil yellow brings instant zing to this bedroom. Mustard-yellow walls in a Santa Fe kitchen are the perfect companion for a collection of vintage plates from Oaxaca, Mexico.

TREILLAGE, FROM an Old French word for woven objects, is at its simplest a trelliswork built to support a climbing plant like clematis, ivy, or a rambling rose. No less a design eminence than Elsie de Wolfe recommended bringing the trellis indoors in her 1913 opus, *The House in Good Taste*, and the word *treillage* now generally refers to wooden latticework (real or illusory) that's been applied to painted walls or overlaid on mirrors to create a room with the carefree mood of a summer garden.

Fanciful trelliswork sets off floral fabric and avian figurines while arched windows pour in the sunlight. It's a delightful folly of a room, more indigenous to the Cotswold countryside than its actual location—a brand-new house in Dallas.

CLOCKWISE FROM TOP LEFT A foyer festooned with intricate mint-green trelliswork brings a touch of the Brighton Pavilion to a Bahamas vacation house. The dark ground of this coastal Rhode Island dining room's trellis wallpaper gives it a 3-D effect. A playful poolside chinoiserie pagoda in Palm Beach is furnished with garden furniture that disappears into its lattice walls. Simply adding trelliswork to this tiny throwaway space at the end of an entry hall makes it a beautiful bridge to the gardens outside.

Transforming a dark upstairs hall into a sparkling maze, trellis wallpaper combines with mirrors that trick the eye into believing there are additional windows and doors.

"THE MOOR'S LAST SIGH" refers to the heartbroken departure in 1492 of the sultan Boabdil from his reign over Andalusian Spain. What remained behind, though, was a wealth of Arabic art and architecture that still graces Spanish cities like Córdoba and Grenada. And, of course, a short hop across the Straits of Gibraltar lies the motherlode of Moorish style in the colorfully tiled mosques and meandering medinas of Morocco. What other style of décor has so thoroughly entranced generations of designers?

In a Florida vacation home, a striking Moroccan tile fireplace invigorates this living room. It's the indisputable star of the space.

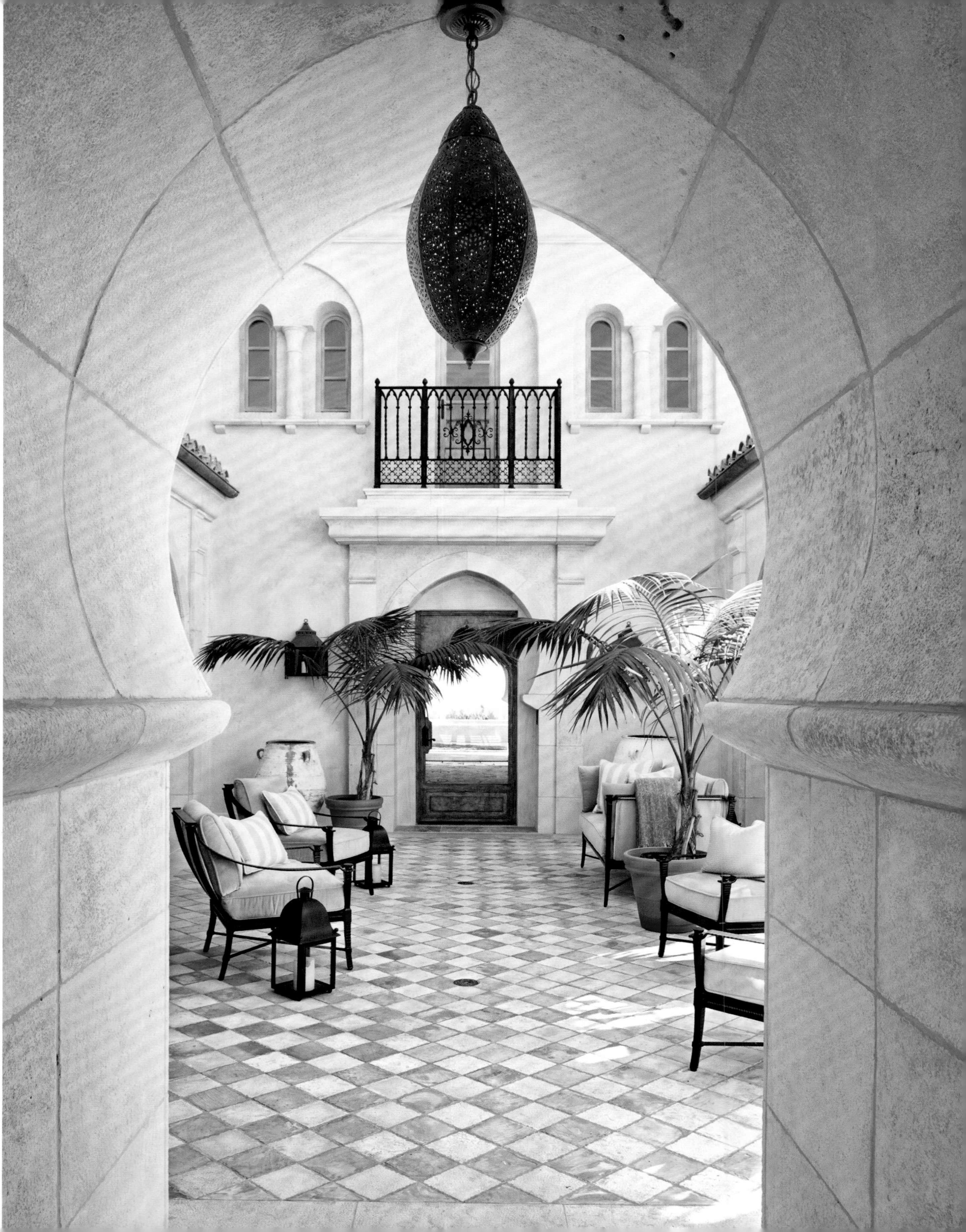

OPPOSITE Moorish arches frame the central courtyard of a new coastal California house with a look that was already classic when Hannibal sacked Rome. The terracotta tile floor, wrought iron parapet, and pierced brass lantern add touchstones of Moroccan style.

THIS PAGE This master bedroom is as lush as a Bedouin princess's tent. The daybed's fabrics have a hand-dyed, straight-from-the-souk look and the inlaid table features mother-of-pearl patterns as ancient as the Sahara.

LEFT Moroccan-style wallpaper surrounds this Pacific Palisades dining table—all that's missing is fresh mint tea.

ABOVE The lacy honeycomb of brass Moroccan lanterns dominates a room fit for a pasha's feast.

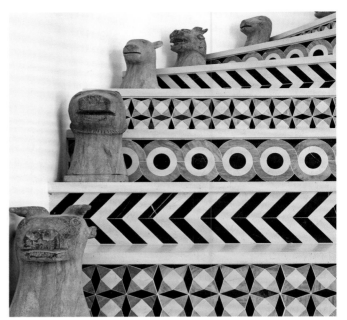

CLOCKWISE FROM TOP LEFT The pairing of a timeworn tile motif and the gleam of brass make an upstate New York kitchen look fresh and young. A staircase becomes a high-stepping art installation with its staggered progression of Moroccan tile patterns. An etched brass tray table brings a touch of history to a new home's outdoor terrace. With its flamboyant tiled floor and arched shower doorway, this bath could easily be found tucked into some charming little *riad* in Rabat.

The intricate patterns of overblown lotus leaves and a tribal-inspired rug intersect in a young girl's North African–inflected bedroom. A sequined Moroccan wedding blanket draped across the bed is the capping touch.

LEFT The traditional geometric imagery of Moroccan tile mosaics inspires the ceiling and border of this pool house. Artisans painted it on beadboard for a (literally) over-the-top, tent-like effect.

ABOVE Moorish architecture and oceanfront homes are a pairing made in paradise. At this white-stuccoed Santa Barbara beauty, the California seaside views could as easily be the exotic Barbary Coast.

PHOTOGRAPHY CREDITS

FRONT COVER: Annie Schlechter

BACK COVER (clockwise from top right): Annie Schlechter, Eric Piasecki, Douglas Friedman, Trevor Tondro

William Abranowicz: 31 (top), 66, 94–95, 100, 246 (top right), 246 (bottom right)

Melanie Acevedo: 70–71, 86, 110–111, 192–193, 238 (bottom right)

Mali Azima: 57

James Baigrie: 24, 106 (bottom left), 214–215, 243

Christopher Baker: 121 (bottom right), 148, 165, 248

Edmund Barr: 1

Roland Bello: 17 (top left), 20–21, 44 (top left)

John Gould Bessler: 145 (top right)

Julien Capmeil: 154

Paul Costello: 4 (top right), 90–91, 238 (bottom left)

Beatriz da Costa: 12 (top left), 58, 121 (top left), 161 (top right), 167 (top left), 167 (top right), 220 (top left)

Roger Davies: 166

Reed Davis: 179

François Dischinger: 128

Brian Doben: 26–27, 92, 93 (bottom left)

Miki Duisterhof: 151, 175

Don Freeman: 69, 149, 183 (top right)

Douglas Friedman: 234

Miguel Flores-Vianna: 17 (bottom left), 78–79, 121 (bottom left), 132 (top left), 161 (bottom right), 228–229, 236

Mick Hales: 48–49

Nelson Hancock: 158–159, 178

Alec Hemer: 196

Ditte Isager: 197

Thibault Jeanson: 213

John Kernick: 132 (bottom left)

Nathan Kirkman: 106 (top right)

Francesco Lagnese: 4 (bottom left), 31 (bottom), 42–43, 54–55, 64 (top left), 64 (top right), 67, 75 (bottom right), 93 (bottom right), 113 (bottom right), 123, 132 (bottom right), 152, 180, 181 (bottom right), 184–185, 188, 191, 203 (top left), 231, 238 (top right), 239, 252

David A. Land: 11, 108, 125, 240

Pernille Loof: 116–117

Thomas Loof: 4 (top left), 4 (bottom right), 7, 12 (bottom right), 13, 17 (bottom right), 18, 22–23, 29, 52, 68, 84, 97, 104–105, 122, 124 (top left), 137, 167 (bottom left), 174 (top left), 203 (bottom right), 216, 238 (top left)

Maura McEvoy: 16, 50–51, 62, 82, 113 (bottom left), 126–127, 138, 174 (bottom right), 206, 212, 247

James Merrell: 60–61, 64 (bottom left), 75 (bottom left), 93 (top left), 124 (bottom left), 129, 156–157, 161 (bottom left), 186 (top right), 186 (bottom right), 194–195, 204, 219, 220 (top right)

Karyn Millet: 101 (bottom left), 132 (top right), 181 (top left), 222–223

Ngoc Minh Ngo: 17 (top right), 87, 93 (top right), 164, 174 (top left), 174 (bottom left), 218, 235 (top left)

Peter Murdock: 124 (top left), 176–177, 200, 203 (top right)

Amy Neunsinger: 31 (middle), 38–39, 44 (bottom left), 203 (bottom left), 242, 244

Victoria Pearson: 28, 120, 134, 139 (top right), 139 (bottom left), 143, 145 (bottom right), 172, 190, 230

Eric Piasecki: 12 (top right), 12 (bottom left), 33, 34–35, 65, 72, 75 (top left), 80–81, 101 (top right), 102, 115, 142, 145 (top left), 146, 147, 181 (top right), 205, 207

Eric Piasecki/Otto Archive: 32

José Picayo: 99, 221

Paul Raeside: 75 (top right), 98, 124 (bottom right), 139 top left, 160, 198, 211, 220 (bottom left), 226–227

Laura Resen: 170–171, 208–209

Marco Ricca: 139

Lisa Romerein: 44 (top right), 73, 74, 150, 155, 181 (bottom left), 235

Annie Schlechter: 10, 19, 46, 47, 88, 96 (top right), 96 (bottom right), 112, 118, 187, 224

Joe Schmelzer: 107

James Ray Spahn: 106 (top left)

Tim Street-Porter: 53

Christopher Sturman: 25, 40–41, 101 (top left), 167 (bottom right)

Trevor Tondro: 83, 114, 173, 186 (top right), 186 (bottom left), 245, 246 (top left), 246 (bottom left)

Luca Trovato: 201

David Tsay: 106 (bottom right), 113 (top right)

Simon Upton: 44 (bottom right), 136

Jonny Valiant: 14, 45, 101 (bottom right), 113 (top left), 133, 144, 145 (bottom left), 161 (top left), 169, 183 (top left), 183 (bottom left), 189, 202, 232–233

Mikkel Vang: 249

Peter Vitale: 235 (bottom left)

William Waldron: 56

Bjorn Wallander: 8, 30, 36, 63, 96 (top left), 119, 131, 168, 182, 210, 220 (bottom right), 225

Simon Watson: 64 bottom left, 76–77, 85, 96 (bottom left), 235 (top right)

Julian Wass: 15, 140–141, 162

Luke White: 2, 183 (bottom right)

Leslie Williamson: 121 (top right), 130

INTERIOR DESIGN CREDITS

FRONT COVER: Suellen Gregory; *BACK COVER* (clockwise from top right): Suellen Gregory, Steven Gambrel, Tilton Fenwick; *PAGE 1:* Suzanne Tucker; *PAGE 2:* Summer Thornton; *PAGE 4* (clockwise from top left): Amanda Lindroth, Jane Scott Hodges, Jeffrey Bilhuber, Bunny Williams; *PAGE 7:* Ellen O'Neill; *PAGE 8:* Mark D. Sikes; *PAGE 10:* Gary McBournie; *PAGE 11:* Sam Allen; *PAGE 12* (clockwise from top left): Michelle Adams, Kay Douglass, Amanda Lindroth, Kay Douglass; *PAGE 13:* Amanda Lindroth; *PAGE 14:* Christina Murphy Pisa & Nina Carbone; *PAGE 15:* Jeffrey Bilhuber; *PAGE 16:* Nick Olsen; *PAGE 17* (clockwise from top left): Miles Redd, David Kaihoi, Kari McCabe (Architect: Nate McBride), Cathy Kincaid; *PAGE 18:* Christopher Maya; *PAGE 19:* Gary McBournie; *PAGES 20–21:* Miles Redd; *PAGES 22–23:* Amanda Lindroth; *PAGE 24:* Caitlin Moran; *PAGE 25:* Celerie Kemble; *PAGES 26–27:* Philip Gorrivan; *PAGE 28:* Erin Martin; *PAGE 30:* Mark D. Sikes; *PAGE 31* (from top): Susanna Salk, Peter Dunham, Lindsey Coral Harper; *PAGE 32:* Gideon Mendelson; *PAGE 33:* Steven Gambrel; *PAGES 34–35:* Steven Gambrel; *PAGE 36:* Amanda Lindroth; *PAGES 38–39:* Mary McDonald; *PAGES 40–41:* Bill Brockschmidt & Courtney Coleman; *PAGES 42–43:* Tom Scheerer; *PAGE 44* (clockwise from top left): Miles Redd, Benjamin Dhong, Celerie Kemble & Caroline Irvin of Kemble Interiors, Marie Nygren & Smith Hanes; *PAGE 45:* Christina Murphy Pisa & Nina Carbone; *PAGES 46–47:* Suellen Gregory; *PAGES 48–49:* Charles O. Schwarz III; *PAGES 50–51:* Nick Olsen; *PAGE 52:* Sally Markham; *PAGE 53:* Martyn Lawrence Bullard; *PAGES 54–55:* Myra Hoefer; *PAGE 56:* Timothy Whealon; *PAGE 57:* Tammy Connor; *PAGE 58:* Ashley Whittaker; *PAGES 60–61:* Justine Cushing; *PAGE 62:* Lilly Bunn; *PAGE 63:* Mark D. Sikes; *PAGE 64* (clockwise from top left): Melissa Rufty, Meg Braff, Todd Klein, Robert Southern; *PAGE 65:* Kay Douglass; *PAGE 66:* Betsy Brown; *PAGE 67:* Meg Braff; *PAGE 68:* Bunny Williams; *PAGE 69:* Susan Ferrier; *PAGES 70–71:* Mimi McMakin & Ashley Sharpe of

Kemble Interiors; *PAGE 72:* Steven Gambrel; *PAGE 73:* Benjamin Dhong; *PAGE 74:* Benjamin Dhong; *PAGE 75* (clockwise from top left): Katie Ridder, Garrow Kedigian, Susan Ferrier, Miles Redd; *PAGES 76–77:* Jeannette Whitson; *PAGES 78–79:* Lisa Fine; *PAGES 80–81:* Architecture and design by Ruard Veltman; *PAGE 82:* Colleen Bashaw; *PAGE 83:* Erin Martin; *PAGE 84:* Melanie Pounds; *PAGE 85:* Jeannette Whitson; *PAGE 86:* Meyer Davis Studio; *PAGE 87:* Lindsey Coral Harper; *PAGE 88:* Suellen Gregory; *PAGES 90–91:* Jane Scott Hodges; *PAGE 92:* Philip Gorrivan; *PAGE 93* (clockwise from top left): Frank Roop, Phoebe Howard, Lindsey Coral Harper, Philip Gorrivan; *PAGES 94–95:* Betsy Burnham; *PAGE 96* (clockwise from top left): Jill Sharp Weeks, Robert Stilin, Lili O'Brien & Leigh Anne Muse, Bill Ingram; *PAGE 97:* Elizabeth Tyler Kennedy; *PAGE 98:* Garrow Kedigian; *PAGE 99:* Andrew Raquet; *PAGE 100:* Betsy Burnham; *PAGE 101* (clockwise from top left): Celerie Kemble, Kureck Jones, Tracery Interiors, Tobi Tobin; *PAGES 102–103:* Steven Gambrel; *PAGES 104–105:* Elizabeth Tyler Kennedy; *PAGE 106* (clockwise from top left): Architect William Hefner, Frank Ponterio, Justina Blakeney, Caitlin Moran; *PAGE 107:* John De Bastiani; *PAGE 108:* Andrew Howard; *PAGES 110–111:* Mimi McMakin & Ashley Sharpe of Kemble Interiors; *PAGE 112:* Suellen Gregory; *PAGE 113* (clockwise from top left): Fawn Galli, Justina Blakeney, Sara Gilbane, Colleen Bashaw; *PAGE 114:* Tilton Fenwick; *PAGE 115:* Katie Ridder; *PAGES 116–117:* Laurie Blumenfeld-Russo; *PAGE 118:* Leslie Klotz; *PAGE 119:* Jill Sharp Weeks; *PAGE 120:* Erin Martin; *PAGE 121* (clockwise from top left): Ashley Whittaker, Mackay Boynton, Justine Cushing & Pauline Pitt & Eugene Niven Goodman, Lisa Fine; *PAGE 122:* Christopher Maya; *PAGE 123:* Tom Scheerer; *PAGE 124* (clockwise from top left): Janet Gregg, Ashley Whittaker, Catherine Brown Paterson, Todd Romano; *PAGE 125:* Sam Allen; *PAGES 126–127:* Philip Gorrivan; *PAGE 128:* Steven Sclaroff; *PAGE 129:* Kathryn M. Ireland; *PAGE 130:* Mackay Boynton; *PAGE 131:* John Knott &

John Fondas; *PAGE 132* (clockwise from top left): Lisa Fine, Massucco Warner Miller, Eliza Dyson, Annie Selke; *PAGE 133:* Barry Dixon; Design Aurore by Paule Marrot 1949 Exclusive copyright Paule Marrot Ed Paris SAS; *PAGE 134:* Frances Merrill; *PAGE 136:* Celerie Kemble & Caroline Irvin of Kemble Interiors; *PAGE 137:* Alex Papachristidis; *PAGE 138:* Colleen Bashaw; *PAGE 139* (clockwise from top left): Catherine Brown Paterson, Frances Merrill, Bennett Leifer, Nathan Turner; *PAGE 140–141:* Jeffrey Bilhuber; *PAGE 142:* Katie Ridder; *PAGE 143:* Windsor Smith; *PAGE 144:* Richard Keith Langham; *PAGE 145* (clockwise from top left): Gideon Mendelson, T. Keller Donovan, Chris Barrett, Jean-Louis Deniot; *PAGES 146–147:* Eleanor Cummings; *PAGE 148:* Susan Ferrier of McAlpine Booth & Ferrier Interiors; *PAGE 149:* Susan Ferrier; *PAGE 150:* Benjamin Dhong; *PAGE 151:* Doug Davis & Hannon Kirk Doody; *PAGES 152–153:* Lindsey Coral Harper; *PAGE 154:* Kristin Kong; *PAGE 155:* Benjamin Dhong; *PAGES 156–157:* Meg Braff; *PAGES 158–159:* Bruce Shostak; *PAGE 160:* Tom Samet & Ross Meltzer; *PAGE 161* (clockwise from top left): Christina Murphy Pisa & Nina Carbone, Ashley Whittaker, Gregory Shano, Meg Braff; *PAGE 162:* Aaron Hom; *PAGE 165:* Markham Roberts; *PAGE 166:* Joe Nye; *PAGE 167* (clockwise from top left): Michelle Adams, Lindsey Coral Harper, Bill Brockschmidt & Courtney Coleman, Justine Cushing; *PAGE 168:* Jill Sharp Weeks; *PAGE 169:* Zim Loy; *PAGES 170–171:* Antonio Martins & John Mayberry; *PAGE 172:* Schuyler Samperton; *PAGE 173:* Tilton Fenwick; *PAGE 174* (clockwise from top left): Jeffrey Bilhuber, Ken Fulk, Philip Gorrivan, Ken Fulk; *PAGE 175:* Ramsay Gourd; *PAGES 176–177:* Miles Redd; *PAGE 178:* Bruce Shostak; *PAGE 179:* Ann Wolf; *PAGE 180:* Eliza Dyson; *PAGE 181* (clockwise from top left): Matt O'Dorisio, Thom Filicia, Eliza Dyson, Thomas Callaway; *PAGE 182:* Jill Sharp Weeks; *PAGE 183* (clockwise from top left): Fawn Galli, Betsy Brown, Marshall Watson, Lindsey Bond; *PAGES 184–185:* Frank Delledonne; *PAGE 186* (clockwise from top left): Erin Martin, Frank Roop, Kathryn M. Ireland, Erin Martin; *PAGE 187:*

Robert Stilin; *PAGE 188:* Martin Horner; *PAGE 189:* Harry Heissmann; *PAGE 190:* Myra Hoefer; *PAGE 191:* Tom Scheerer; *PAGES 192–193:* Meyer Davis Studio; *PAGES 194–195:* Libby Cameron; *PAGE 196:* Kim Dempster & Erin Martin; *PAGE 197:* Harriet Maxwell Macdonald & Andrew Corrie; *PAGE 198:* Amy Lau; *PAGE 200:* Amir Khamneipur; *PAGE 201:* Stephen Shubel; *PAGE 202:* Eric Cohler; *PAGE 203* (clockwise from top left): Tom Scheerer, Janet Gregg, Susan Ferrier of McAlpine Booth & Ferrier Interiors, Dana Abbott & Kim Fiscus; *PAGE 204:* Robert Southern; *PAGE 205:* Steven Gambrel; *PAGE 206:* Nick Olsen; *PAGES 208–209:* Antonio Martins & John Mayberry; *PAGE 210:* Jill Sharp Weeks; *PAGE 211:* Garrow Kedigian; *PAGE 212:* Nick Olsen; *PAGE 213:* Alessandra Branca; *PAGES 214–215:* Steven Miller; *PAGES 216–217:* Christopher Maya; *PAGE 218:* Elizabeth Pyne; *PAGE 219:* Meg Braff; *PAGE 220* (clockwise from top left): Mary McGee, Todd Romano, Mark D. Sikes, Catherine Brown Paterson; *PAGE 221:* Andrew Raquet; *PAGES 222–223:* Massucco Warner Miller; *PAGE 224:* Suellen Gregory; *PAGE 225:* Katie Ridder; *PAGES 226–227:* Catherine Brown Paterson; *PAGES 228–229:* Lisa Fine; *PAGE 230:* Windsor Smith; *PAGE 231:* Amanda Lindroth; *PAGES 232–233:* Christina Murphy Pisa & Nina Carbone; *PAGE 234:* Krista Ewart; *PAGE 235* (clockwise from top left): Lindsey Coral Harper, Windsor Smith, Benjamin Dhong, Judith Espinar & Jim Deville & Scott Robey; *PAGE 236–237:* Cathy Kincaid; *PAGE 238* (clockwise from top left): Amanda Lindroth, Tom Scheerer, Mimi McMakin & Ashley Sharpe of Kemble Interiors, Sara Ruffin Costello; *PAGE 239:* Tom Scheerer; *PAGE 240–241:* Andrew Howard; *PAGE 242:* Ohara Davies-Gaetano; *PAGE 243:* Caitlin Moran; *PAGE 244:* Mark D. Sikes; *PAGE 245:* Erin Martin; *PAGE 246* (clockwise from top left): Tilton Fenwick, Betsy Burnham, Betsy Burnham, Karen Vidal; *PAGE 247:* Colleen Bashaw; *PAGE 248:* Robin Bell; *PAGE 249:* Christina Rottman; *PAGE 252:* Ashley Whittaker

INDEX

Note: Page numbers indicate caption locations.

EDITOR Rebecca Kaplan

DESIGNER Sarah Gifford

PRODUCTION MANAGER Rebecca Westall

Library of Congress Control Number: 2016960986

ISBN: 978-1-4197-2657-6

Printed and bound in China
10 9 8 7 6 5 4 3 2 1

Abrams books are available at special discounts when purchased in
quantity for premiums and promotions as well as fundraising or educational
use. Special editions can also be created to specification. For details,
contact specialsales@abramsbooks.com or the address below.

ABRAMS The Art of Books
115 West 18th Street, New York, NY 10011
abramsbooks.com

PAGE 1 In a California retreat, a romantic
arbor covered with ivy and wisteria
connects the main house to a pavilion
used solely for dinner parties.

PAGE 2 Moroccan tile enlivens a Florida
lanai and adds to this outdoor living
room's profusion of blue-and-white.

PAGE 4, CLOCKWISE FROM TOP LEFT
A beach house master bedroom gets
a cheerful dose of tangerine. In a
New Orleans powder room, gondola
wallpaper is a nod to Louisiana's small
wood boats called pirogues. A tub
is surrounded by an antique painted
screen for coziness. With a plump
ottoman tucked underneath, this living
room's proper English tea table looks
downright friendly.

PAGE 7 A large-scale toile covers a
daybed and screen creating a snug
sleeping nook in a Manhattan studio
apartment.

PAGE 252 In this waterside home, the
living room's hazy blue palette melds
with the outside in a mood-lifting way.